58 DAYS

A Wilderness Story

MARISSA GOULD

EDITED BY LILIAN DUVAL

58 Days: A Wilderness Story

Published by Wheatmark®
2030 East Speedway Boulevard, Suite 106
Tucson, Arizona 85719 USA
www.wheatmark.com

ISBN: 978-1-62787-480-9 (paperback)
ISBN: 978-1-62787-481-6 (ebook)
LCCN: 2016963141

Contents

When you look back at high school, which year sticks out most in your mind?

Senior year.

Everyone remembers senior year as fun, exciting, and momentous. All the high school movies recount senior-year pranks or senior-year love sagas. Senior year can mean losing your virginity, going to bars with fake IDs, and running from cops at house parties. When everyone goes off to college, the topic of choice for freshman conversation is how amazing everyone's senior year was, and which assholes pulled the craziest shit.

My senior year had, let's say, a slight twist. This is my account of the summer before my senior year, exactly as I remember it, exactly as it felt to be a girl in a nice suburban high school one minute, and a prisoner in a so-called "character-development wilderness program for troubled teens" the next. I got ripped from my life and thrown into the woods, with no warning at all. And I never went back to my high school.

I didn't set out to become an investigative nature reporter, but that was the role I assumed during all those exhausting hikes, insect assaults, forced meals, and episodes of deprivation and humiliation. During all those suffering hours and miserable days that stretched into interminable weeks with no end in sight, I had nothing to call my own—nothing but my thoughts. My words. My journals. And a pair of orange crocs.

If this reminiscence helps only one teenager avoid my fate, or makes just one parent look deeper and hesitate before signing a child's life away, then my mission will have been accomplished. In these pages, you'll experience what I uncovered first-hand about the painful injustices imposed by the industry, and about the cooperation, or collusion, between therapeutic rehabilitation centers and the reform schools they feed. Wilderness programs and reform schools originated as moral ideas, but the reality of these systems is far from their mission statements.

This is what happens when you take kids away from home and lock up all the "at-risk" children of society in a therapeutic boarding school, and tell them that they aren't going home for fifteen months.

This is my senior year. This is my story.

Life is what you make of it.

"Wake up, Marissa." My mom switches the lights on.

I pull the blanket over my head. "I don't have a final today. I got an A in that class. Let me sleep!" I moan from underneath the blanket.

I'm 17, a junior at Tenafly High School in New Jersey, ten minutes from the George Washington Bridge and New York City.

"Come on, you have to wake up." Her voice is cold, removed.

Peeking out from underneath my blanket, half asleep, head aching, I see my mother standing by my bedroom door.

"Wake up, Marissa." It's not her regular weekday wake-up voice.

I unveil my face. Standing at the foot of my bed is a butch woman at least five foot eleven, more than 200 pounds, with short, spiky, pomaded hair. She's dressed all in khakis, staring at me, no expression on her face.

I must be having a nightmare.

Over in the corner there's another oversized stranger in khakis, the number-one hick Billy Bob, with a buzz cut sticking up in a circle on top of his big head. He's the kind of guy you stand away from in a crowd. Big enough to be a bouncer, he's around six feet six, at least 300 pounds. His face is stoic.

My mother and father are standing in my bedroom doorway with somber looks.

My heart pounds when I comprehend that this is real. I'm awake. I shoot upright in bed, staring at myself in the mirror directly across from me. Fully conscious now, I reach under my pillow for my cell phone to call my sort-of boyfriend, Mark, who will know how to get me out of this situation, whatever it is. But my phone is gone.

I glance around the room in a panic. The alarm clock says 3:30 a.m. Have I really been asleep for only an hour?

My parents are blocking me in. What? What are my parents doing in my room with two grim-faced bounty hunters who look like they're about to kill me? What's going on? With a last sliver of hope, I tell myself I'm dreaming. But this feels too real. Tears, loss of air, the gripping feeling of reality. I'm not dreaming. This is real.

"What's going on?" I yell at my parents. "What are you doing to me?"

"You're going to a camp," my mom says.

"What are you talking about? What kind of camp?"

"A wilderness camp."

A wilderness camp? I can't read her face. *What the fuck is going on?* Why on earth are they sending me away five days before I'm supposed to leave for Los Angeles for the summer?

I've been accepted by the UCLA musical theater program, and it's going to be the best summer of my life. The program is for kids who have potential for musical theater, and I've already been in two Broadway shows. I guess most people would be proud, but other kids have always made fun of me for what they call bragging, whenever I said anything about my other life—my life onstage. That's why I've stopped singing in front of friends or classmates altogether. No one at school knows about my early career except for my friends from elementary school days.

My career started at age seven when my parents signed me with Shirley Grant Management. At eight, I appeared in several national commercials, in an Actors' Equity performance, and in "The Sound of Music" on Broadway. At ten, I booked more big-name commercials, sang on the video series "Drew's Famous Magical Jukebox," and played a major role in "A Christmas Carol" at Madison Square Garden. My mom and dad didn't push me at all. This was what I wanted to do. I was lucky that I could sing, dance, and act; and for a few years, I was the happiest kid in the world.

UCLA is my dream college. I'm worried whether my good grades and extra-curriculars aren't enough to get me admitted. To be accepted, I'll need an interview; it's what I'm good at—talking to people. In high school, I've done only cheerleading, and I've gone on auditions; I'm not a club kid or a community service kid. So I'm going to this summer program looking to make great networking connections with the professors who I hope will be teaching me next year as a freshman. I want early-decision admission more than anything, and I've been working on it for years. To the land of dreams I want to go! It's where I feel that I'm meant to be.

I catch my mom's eye. "What? I'm going to California in a week; I can't go to any wilderness camp."

"You don't have a choice," she says. "You're going to Adirondack Leadership Expeditions in upstate New York. You're not going to California anymore."

I'm frozen in bed and don't want to move. "For how long?" *I don't have time for this*, I say to myself. Somewhere inside, I think that once I get up and do what they say, I'll be locked in and screwed.

My dad is just standing there silently, eyes wide, taking in everything but saying nothing.

"Four to six weeks," my mom answers. She looks away as one of the gorillas at the foot of my bed interrupts.

"You have to say goodbye now," the guy orders. "Your parents have to leave and we need to get going."

"Mom! Don't do this! Mom, please stop this!" I beg. "This will change everything, forever!" I don't know exactly what's happening, but I know that I'll never look at them the same way again, will never feel the same about them again. "If you walk out the door, you'll lose me forever."

She looks away as if she's been practicing for this moment.

"Nothing's going to be the same again. You don't want to do this," I keep saying. She's not answering me.

The thug takes half a step forward, closer to my bed. "We can do this the hard way, or you can just listen to what we have to say and you can comply."

Comply? Is he sure my parents aren't going to change their minds? Is he getting tired of hearing me plead with them, as if I'm wasting his time? Straining my eyes and pulling my fingers through my hair, I have nowhere to turn. Tears are pouring like waterfalls from my eyes. *What the fuck is going on?* I'm stunned and hyperventilating.

The hillbillies try to calm me down. "You need to breathe. Deep, long, slow breaths," they advise.

"What are you doing to me, Mom? What are you doing?"

"Say goodbye now," the tough-looking woman commands.

I don't move. I sit upright on my bed wearing only my underwear and a T-shirt with the name of a local band, Cross-Fire. No words. Just tears.

"Call Mark for me," I ask my mom.

"I will." She's not looking me in the eye; she's looking around the room instead.

Every horrible emotion that I didn't believe existed, I'm feeling right now. I'd never known depression, never looked it in the face—that would come later, in the wilderness. For now, I'm in physical pain. I don't know what to think or what to feel or what to say, or even if I know these people whom I called parents until this moment.

I look at my mom, straight-eyed and serious. "If you go through with this, our relationship will never be the same," I warn her.

"We love you, Marissa. This will be good for you."

You've just lost your only daughter, I think to myself.

And now they're gone.

My head is blank, for the first time in my life. I do not know how to get out of this mess. My eyes blurry, I look around my room from my computer on the left, then over to my window, through which I couldn't jump even if I tried because it's too high to reach; to my wide mirror propped on the bureau right in front of my bed. Tears of disappointment, shock, and confusion are streaming down my face like a leaking faucet, with black lines of mascara running down with them. My small figure looks helpless and lost in the middle of my queen-sized purple bed. To the right is the door through which my parents left.

The front door alarm beeps. My parents must have left the house after they walked out of my room. They took off and left me with these escorts, with no choice but to obey them.

I'm half naked, sitting on my bed, confused, with so many questions unanswered.

The man sees me watching the door and gives a stern look to the woman, who steps over to block my way. "You don't want to run," she cautions me. "It wouldn't help this situation. Your parents signed away your rights to us and we have control over you right now."

My parents signed my rights away? What on earth were they thinking? I start to panic again. My face contorts with an appalled look on it; I see it in the mirror.

"We aren't going to hurt you," the guy says. "We just want you to come with us. We don't want to have to restrain you."

"*Restrain* me?" I ask with wide-open eyes.

"Yes, restrain you."

I'm shocked, betrayed, and confused. Betrayed over all; beyond blind-sighted. There are two of them and one of me, me in undies at five feet tall and 95 pounds. Running away doesn't even cross my mind. I know they're not going to hurt me. The rational part of my brain figures that my parents probably paid a lot of money for this ridiculousness, and I have to go. I'm 17. I'm fucked. I have no rights at all.

I never thought that my mother would do anything like this. My dad is not very emotional, so I never gave him much thought, but my mom, I speak to her all the time, and she drives me to school every day. It's her workplace too—she's the substance abuse counselor at Tenafly High School.

I ended up a student at the school where my mother works because Tenafly is close to New York City where I was working as a child performer on Broadway. We lived in another town more than an hour away before I entered fifth grade. From Tenafly, Mom could drive me over the George Washington Bridge to the city whenever I needed to be there, which was often.

I had a choice before fifth grade to either be in my mother's school district or give up acting.

I chose Tenafly, and we all moved there—our small family: my mom, my dad, and me.

My parents complain that I'm unmanageable, disrespectful, unruly, and going nowhere. Typical parent-teen conflict. This translates to me as *I'm not good enough for them*. Once I was no longer booking big gigs on Broadway, or getting one national commercial after another, show after show, there were no more acclamations, no more "Look, that's our daughter, she's amazing." Instead, it was, "Yeah, she's doing her thing these days." I was no longer their ideal of perfection. I was no longer good enough for them.

But I never expected this. They'd threatened me about the hospital and psych wards before, but those were threats with no backing. Then one day I wake up to this, and I'm gone.

I look at my closet, full of brightly colored clothes, with so many of my secrets locked away in its corners. My purse is within reach on the floor slightly under my bed, containing my cigarettes, rolling papers, and a red, white, and blue piece, which I named Amsterdam after the place where I first smoked out of it. And my car! There's a Xanax bar stowed away in my locked glove compartment. Various pills might be inside an Advil bottle in my center console—Percocets, codeines, Concerta, Adderall, Klonopins. What about the CD rack right next to me, where I used to conceal empty bags of cocaine under CDs in their cases? Had I forgotten some empty bags after I stopped using cocaine?

Cascades of worries are firing all at once, exploding in my brain like the Fourth of July fireworks finale. But I guess it doesn't matter anymore. Everything is completely out of my control and I don't know what is going to happen to me next and I certainly can't say to these escorts, "Hey, excuse me while I go hide my drugs and paraphernalia." I'm SOL—shit out of luck—and up a goddamn creek without a paddle, that's for damn sure.

I shoot another look at the clock: 3:45 a.m. This all started 15 minutes ago.

"You can grab your iPod for the drive if you want," the man says.

"It's in my car," I answer, but I know that's out of the picture. They're certainly not going to trust me to get my keys, open my car, and get out my iPod while getting escorted to a wilderness program in God-knows-where.

I bought my treasured Acura TSX 07 brand new, in black-on-black leather, and paid in cash with all my own money that I'd earned through my acting career over the years. I walked in with a check written to cash and walked out with a car that my father refused to put in my name for "insurance purposes." It's an ongoing controversy between us. I always argue, if I want to go somewhere, I can because I paid for the car myself and it's not fair to restrict me from something that I purchased myself, for my own freedom. My car symbolizes freedom to me. I can go where I want; I'm not confined; I can drive cross-country if I want. No car means I am stuck relying on others, mainly my parents.

Back to reality. "Can I get dressed and take off my makeup?"

"Yes, but we need to watch you, for precautionary measures," the guy answers.

These Gigantors are going to watch me get dressed when I'm already half naked. Great, just fucking great.

Whatever, it doesn't matter anymore anyway, I sigh to myself. I get out of bed and walk slowly to my dresser to put on a pair of sweatpants and a different T-shirt. From the closet I snatch a sweatshirt and a pair of UGGs. It may be June 20 and 80 degrees outside, but I still want to be comfortable.

"Can I wear any jewelry there?"

"I think so, only a few small things," the woman says. (This would turn out to be a lie. They don't know the program because they don't work there; they're just hired hands.)

I keep my pink sapphire and diamond ring on my right-hand ring finger. Since I first acquired it, I've never taken it off. This ring feels like a part of me. I bought it for myself as I do all of my large purchases. It's a reminder that I've always done everything alone, and now, at seventeen, all my control is ripped from me, only nine months before my legal freedom at eighteen.

Face wipes brush away the black lines marking my cheeks from the tears that fell and the tears that are still falling. I get one last look at my captors before we go outside into the darkness. Their clothes don't say "Adirondack Leadership Expeditions," which is where they're taking me. They're not wearing badges or name tags. I find out later that they're not employees of ALE; they're from a separate company that ALE hired to do their dirty work. Mercenaries coming to save me from myself. They're both in tan khakis from head to toe, reminding me of what the staff of an insane asylum would wear.

I suck myself up and turn after the kidnappers, who walk me out of my room, into the hall, down the steps, and out my front door for the last time in what will turn out to be more than nine months.

It's still dark outside but light enough to see a teal-colored Mercury, maybe a 2004, parked at the end of the driveway. The goons walk me to the car, open the back door, and motion for me to get in. The Amazon woman slides in next to me on the back seat, which is tan and velvety; it feels like it's been sat on over and over again. It sags with the weight of me and the butch woman, much like an old couch that's lost its spring. Probably it's a safety concern to let me sit in the back seat by myself. It wouldn't look good for their company if I somehow figured out a way to get out of the car and fall out the door while on the highway. Kids getting injured or killed while being escorted, I'm sure wouldn't look good.

The other ogre gets in the front seat, starts the car, and backs away from the nice suburban New Jersey house where it all started.

THE DRIVE

For most of the five-hour car ride I don't speak to either of the escorts. I watch the familiar highways and roads pass me by until they recede into mere memories. Lush green trees lining the road whiz past. The familiar scent of approaching summer fades away, replaced by a piney, cedar-like smell as we drive farther north. We drive, and the sights grow less familiar; we drive, and my tears dry up, my breath starts to calm. It's a long ride, but five hours seems like one hour because of all the memories of home flooding into my mind. I sit in the car, silent, angry about what I'm going to miss, and wondering what exactly my parents were thinking when they committed me to this. How could they think this was the right course of action? *Maybe it won't be so bad*, I try to tell myself with some last glimmers of hope.

Before the guy who's driving got into the car, he handed me a pad of paper and a pen and told me I could write letters to my friends and family, and they'll be passed on to my parents. I take out the pad now and write down a list of names I want my parents to call. Then I write nine letters to all the people I care about in the life I was leading before I was taken.

None of which will make it anywhere past a garbage can once I leave that car. The letter-writing activity is a sham, like much of what will follow. It's nothing more than busywork to keep a captive teenager quiet, to calm her down by any means possible, even if they are lying.

Starting to connect the dots now, I see that my mother's behavior in the past week makes a lot more sense. The phone call I got from my mom fifteen minutes before my curfew that night. (She was making sure I hadn't figured it out somehow and run away.) How nice my mom was to me the day before. The ignored fights, the turned heads while I was smoking pot in my room in the preceding weeks. The reason they kept putting off getting me a new cell phone before I left for L.A., all because they knew I would never use it. This whole scene was planned. One thing I never thought my parents capable of, has come harshly true. They betrayed all of the trust I had in them. They plotted, they manipulated, they lied, and then they sent me away.

The Mercury pulls onto a small dirt road marked by a skinny wooden pole with a brightly colored plastic tie on top. As the car chugs up the road, a white house and small campground come into view. Four wooden benches are arranged in a square to the right of the building, with a group of six boys in prison-like attire sitting on them.

The man pulls the car into the parking lot to the left of the building. Popping his head around from the front, he announces, "We're here." Where I'm going to spend the next four to, I'm not sure, maybe six weeks. Or maybe more. I have no idea.

The Infirm

Getting out of the car and stepping on the dirt surrounding the white building, I take a look around. Slowly turning 360 degrees, I try to soak it all in. I'm in the middle of eastern bumblefuck. What the hell am I going to do?

The one thing Mark has always tried to teach me is diplomacy. Do what I have to do to get by. Say what people want to hear, and do what I don't want to do if it's going to get me to where I want to be. It's politics, he says. I miss him already.

I am working on it, but my problems with authority began when I was working at such a young age. I truly believe that adolescents and adults should have equal authority when communicating, which is an attitude I will have to leave behind, and quick, if I plan to succeed for even one day out here. There is nothing from these people that I want to learn.

From the moment I set foot on the dirt outside this white building, everything that I do or say will be a means to an end. I am being watched with every step I take. The only way I'm going to gain control of this situation is to tell them what they want to hear. The building in front of me is formally known as the infirmary, but everyone at camp, instructors included, calls it "the infirm" for short.

We proceed around the back of the building and up the

winding stairs into a small room where a woman is sitting and staring at me openly, with an unreadable expression. Compared to the woman who escorted me, she's small— around five foot five, medium weight, dressed in jeans and a T-shirt. She looks strong and fit. Anyone who chooses to live in this part of New York State must be good at camping and not mind doing it.

The room is plain. It has white walls, much like the rest of the structure, with two windows directly opposite the door. On the left is a frame for a cot with no mattress on it. In the right corner is a small round table with two chairs. She is sitting in one of them.

She rises. "Hi, I'm P. How was your ride?" She gestures to the other chair and we both sit down.

"Good, a little shocking, but I'll be okay." I sit there staring at her, waiting for her to offer some clarity on this situation.

She doesn't.

I dive right in. "What's the minimum number of days that kids stay here?"

"Twenty-eight. You will get something called a growth book, which will have skills you must complete in order to move on to the next phase."

P is cold, detached, not sympathetic. She doesn't have time for that. It appears that she doesn't want to deal with me, as much as I don't want to deal with her.

"Phase?" I ask. *Great, let's just get this rolling*, I think.

"Yes, there are four phases: Turtle, Bear, Wolf, and Hawk," she recites rapidly. "You start as a Turtle, where you will meet your group and become accustomed to what you do on a daily basis. Then in a few days you become a Bear. Bear phase is where you do the majority of your soft skills and hard skills."

"Soft skills and hard skills?" I raise a questioning eye.

"Soft skills are your emotional growth, and hard skills are

physically making things and learning to start fires, and so on. The rest I'm going to let you figure out for yourself."

It turns out that hard skills are anything we have to make or do with our own hands, such as whittling walking sticks, building traps, sparking fires, and so on. Soft skills are your emotional side that you're working on to progress through the program. They include therapy sessions, which deal with overcoming your problems; and writing exercises related to emotions. If your soft skills aren't improving, only your hard skills, you can't move on to the next phase.

I'm trying to pull as much information out of P as I possibly can so I'll have an edge once I enter my group. I'm sure tons of kids have tried the same thing. Her answers are short and to the point, with no room for more questions, as if she's repeated this scene many time before. At this point, I'm not getting any more answers. Very soon I'll discover that this is their way—you don't need to know anything unless it is *necessary*. Questions like the time of day, where we are headed, how long the hikes are, if we're moving campsites, are all *unnecessary* questions in the program, and answers are not given.

One more try: "Do parents ever come pick up their kids, realizing it's not good for them?"

"No." Firmly.

"Well, I plan on getting right to work and making it out of here in 28 days. I am a very motivated person." I sit up straight with this comment, asserting confidence.

"Well, I'm sure you are. I have never seen anyone graduate here in the allotted minimum 28 days, but I wish you the best of luck," she says with undisguised sarcasm. She gets up and comes over from behind her side of the table.

Great, I think. *P sucks. What a bitch. How hard could it be really?*

She's not done with me yet. "Before you leave this room

and start to get going, we need to outfit you and search you. You also need to remove all of your jewelry and piercings."

My head turns at the word "search," even though I have nothing to be taken away. But this meeting with P is nothing more than a means to an end. I have no choice but to be nice and comply with her to get myself into the first phase, which is one day closer to leaving. My blinders are on.

Still, I say, "But I thought I was allowed to keep some jewelry, some things of importance to me."

"You are allowed only rosary beads," she says.

"But I'm Jewish," I protest.

"Do you have a Star of David you brought that is important to you?"

"No," I answer. She can clearly see that I'm not wearing a Star of David.

"Then you aren't allowed to keep any of what you have," she says.

And that's that.

Reluctantly I remove my ring and the two diamond necklaces hanging around my neck.

I take out my bellybutton ring, wondering if that piercing will close up.

"Here are your clothes for today." She hands me a stack. "The rest are in your pack. You can change now."

For the second time today—is this still the same day?—I have to get dressed in front of a complete stranger. I'm not shy about undressing in the locker room for gym or cheerleading, but this feels more than awkward, standing nearly naked in a plain room with a woman I've just met. She's eying me to be sure that I haven't smuggled anything forbidden into camp.

"Can I keep my bra and underpants?"

"No, we provide those as well."

Great.

She unpacks a duffel bag on the table and I get a glimpse of what I'll be wearing in the woods for however long. Laughing only in my head, I see two pairs of bright-red, breathable hiking pants and two ugly gray cotton long-sleeved shirts. Isn't it summer? Rain pants and a red rain jacket, a bright orange fleece hoodie, a black fleece jacket (that's not bad), and one pair of black fleece pants. This must be some kind of uniform; it's almost identical to what the boys on the benches were wearing. *I'm gonna pick up all the hot boys in these clothes,* I smile sarcastically to myself, and laugh.

I must be smaller than most of the kids who are here—I'm the kind of kid who's always seated in front for class photos—and I figure that the clothes will be enormous. But except for the creepy underwear, the clothes fit more or less because I can't be tripping over things and potentially hurting myself. That would be a liability. The hiking shoes are my size. As I find out later, this camp is expensive, and they can afford to get the right size shoes for kids, but the clothes they provide are just barely acceptable and have no style. I'm sure my mother gave them my size info while she was preparing for this surprise adventure.

It's only 9:30 a.m. and I haven't slept more than an hour since coming home early this morning. I'm feeling disoriented from running on empty, plus the shock of having awakened to this. It's June 20, a day when I was supposed to be sleeping in. The only thing going on at school today is a final that I don't have to take; students who have an overall A in a class at Tenafly High School are exempt from taking the final. It's a public school, yet very college-oriented. About 30 percent of the students go on to Ivy League schools; and I'm aiming for UCLA. The coursework is so difficult that they follow almost a college rule, "If you already have an A, we aren't going to give you another test if you don't want to take it."

While P is flipping through papers on a clipboard, I'm replaying the last week of my previous life. It was strange:

this whole past week, just before I'm leaving for the UCLA musical theater program, my mother has been acting nicer to me than usual. For one thing, I've always had an earlier curfew than my other friends; I don't know why. Last night I asked her if I could stay at my friend Coral's house till 2 a.m. instead of the usual 1:30, so I could spend time with her before leaving for the entire summer in Los Angeles. And my mom said yes without even arguing.

It was my last night of freedom, and I didn't even know it. Coral and I relaxed, watched TV, and smoked a joint with her brother. Nothing crazy. Her parents were also home. They're Israeli and not uptight, and as long as we're safe in their backyard, they're cool with it.

I came home from Coral's promptly at 2 a.m. I am ALWAYS exactly on time to the minute because my mother is a neurotic Jewish parent and would call me at 2:01 if I was one minute late. Back home, I didn't get the feeling that anything unusual was about to happen. My mom said hi from her room, and she didn't come out of her room. I figured that it was late and she wanted to rest. Now I know it was because she didn't have the guts to look me in the face one last time while holding onto this lie. I went to sleep without bothering to wash off my makeup.

P shoves a backpack toward me from behind the table. "So are you ready to get your pack on and get going?" she asks.

"Pack?" I'm exhausted and my eyes are fluttering shut while I'm sitting here. But I need to take in every last word she's saying. My stay at Adirondack Leadership Expeditions depends on it.

She shows me the hiking pack. The pack that's going to carry my shelter, food, and clothing for the next however many days is enormous, almost the same size as I am. It's got to be more than half my weight. At five feet and a whopping ninety-five pounds, down from a hundred because of a little cocaine use and loss of appetite, how am I going to manage this 60-pound pack?

Well, this is going to be fun. I muster a smile and try to pick up the pack. With one foot in front of the other and all the strength I can gather, I yank the strap as hard as I can. But instead of the pack lifting off the ground, I fly right onto the pack.

"I'm going to help you this time, but you are going to learn to do this on your own soon." P smiles at me.

I'm not amused. I stand there while she hoists the pack onto my back. It feels like there's a car on my shoulders. I'm out of breath just from supporting the damn thing.

"We need to go get you checked out by the doctor before we let you off into the woods. Let's go." P starts out the door while I stagger behind, struggling to follow her. She's in a hurry to get me to the doctor ASAP and then ship me off to my group.

At least I get to be in civilization for another two hours or so before I get sheltered away from society.

"The car is downstairs," she says over her shoulder.

I follow P out of the room and down the same stairs where I'd entered. On the dirt road, a black suburban is parked in the same spot where the Mercury that transported me had been. The goons are gone and the Mercury is nowhere in sight. I'll probably never see those people again in my life. Although that thought is not upsetting to me. Their blank, unsympathetic faces will haunt me for months to come.

P opens the back of the suburban so I can place my pack there. Setting it down feels like I'm taking a person off my back. I step around to the side of the car and slide in. Shocked, as I look to my side, sitting next to me is a boy about my age.

"Hi! I'm Andrew! You new?" He smiles. It's the first genuine smile I've seen, the first warm words I've heard since being taken. I stare at Andrew, who's a bit overweight, which strikes me as odd, considering that in this program, you hike all day. He's got a cane or a walking stick, and he appears to be going to the doctor for his hurt leg. A bad sign. He's wearing a black shirt and glasses, and he's staring back at me in a nice sort of way. I immediately feel comfortable seeing another person, and I want to find out from him what I'm in for.

"Um yeah, I just got here, my name's Marissa."

"Where are you from, Marissa?"

"New Jersey, right outside of Manhattan."

"Cool, I'm from Florida. So what did you do to get yourself here?" He smiles again.

"Well, I'm not exactly sure. I know what my parents would say, but I don't agree with them. I smoked a lot of pot and I got arrested." It's no big secret; I don't mind telling him.

"Arrested, well... For what?"

"A zip, an ounce of weed," I tell him, "On the Palisades Parkway. It wasn't my pot, but the kid who was driving the car refused to claim it, so we both got arrested."

Up front, P and the man in the driver's seat occasionally look back through the rearview mirror, trying to catch everything we're saying. I have a feeling that from now on, nothing I say will be private anymore.

From the corner of my eye, I catch Andrew mouthing something to me. Squinting, I try to read his lips.

"Beware of the..."

"What?"

"Beware of the impact letters," he whispers.

"What's an impact letter?"

"You'll see," he explains, "They're from your parents, or so they say. Personally I think the therapists write most of them."

"Therapists?" Andrew is spewing this disjointed information at me very quickly, making it all rather confusing.

"Yeah, you'll get one when you get into your group," Andrew says. I wish he could be in my group; then I would start out with at least one friend.

"OK. What about the phases?" I ask.

"Well, Turtle is only like three days at max, but Bear is next and that's the longest. They make you do a bunch of unnecessary bullshit that you will never need to know again, just to keep you occupied for a long time. Traps are the hardest."

"Traps?" I try to whisper as softly as possible. Eyes from the front seat are on us.

"You'll see, they're a pain," he says. "Fires are OK. But once you're done with all the busywork they give you, you move onto Wolf, which is normally a lot shorter. Then Hawk is the last phase and you're normally in that only for a few days before you graduate and leave."

Andrew pauses only for a second and takes a deep breath. "There are also truth circles, which we have at night. Before they put us to sleep we all have to sit around the fire and talk about something of importance. There is normally a topic, or an activity, or an impact letter. You'll learn more about that when you actually have one. There are also these dumb 'I feel' statements." He shakes his head. "They're crap. You have to say, 'I feel-------, I imagine I feel this way because-------, in the future I hope to----------.' These are a pain in the ass because you have to follow the format and you are required to do a million of them. But you get used to it." Now he's talking in a normal tone of voice.

"Andrew, stop telling her all about the program," P barks from the passenger seat. "She will have to figure it out on her own like everyone else." Her stare shoots right at us through the rearview mirror.

We've been muffled, and I never get to find out why Andrew is here, stuck in this miserable camp.

"OK, OK, I just wanted to help her out a bit," he says.

"She doesn't need help," P snaps.

As soon as she looks away, Andrew leans over to whisper, "The only way you will get yourself out of here is if you give them what they want to hear. Never give up, always be the first to help, and smile when you're asked to do something. Get all your shit straightened out, hike strong, and try not to show weakness, only when it's necessary for them to believe that you are moving past something tough."

"I want to make it out of here in 28 days," I tell him desperately.

"Good luck, chick, I've been here for thirty-four and I'm still a Bear."

The car stops and we're hustled into separate rooms in the doctor's office. I never see Andrew again.

Day 1

WOLF'S DEN

After the doctor visit, P and I get into the black suburban, and she says she's going to hike me to ground camp, whatever that is. The car pulls back into the infirm parking lot surrounded by dirt and rocks. The six boys who'd been sitting on the benches when I first arrived are now gone. I walk around to the back of the car to grab my oversized pack, which I'm not sure I'll be able to carry. I'm right. As I slip the pack onto my back and try to straighten up, the weight throws me backward onto the ground with a hard thud.

"You OK, Marissa?" P asks. "The packs are always a little heavy." She smirks, as if this is a routine conversation that happens daily.

Yeah, right, a little heavy.

I wonder how comical she thinks this is, considering she's gone through this with so many new kids in the program.

"Try leaning forward some," she advises. "Be ready to walk." She bounces past me as if we're doing something fun. Fun for her maybe.

Walking anywhere with this enormous pack will be miserable, but I put on a smile anyway, as Andrew told me, and get ready to hike. Hooking the straps around my waist and adjusting the backpack, I clip the snaps together to get the pack sitting comfortably on my hips. I follow P past the infirm and onto a dirt road, down an embankment of sand, down a slope, and onto a trail leading straight into the trees as far as the eye can see.

The pack's weight on my hips and shoulders is already stressing the muscles in my shoulders and waist, pulling me backward. Even though I've been hiking no more than three minutes, the pain is almost unbearable, and it gets worse every step I take. I wince in pain, forcing myself to keep walking. I know what I have to do: just deal with it. But I can't keep up with P and need to take lots of breaks because I'm not used to the pack, which is burdening me much more than my lack of sleep.

The trail leads to a small clearing and an adjacent path lined with dry gray sticks. Beyond the sticks and wood that mark the boundaries of the trail, there's tall grass, light green and thick, that looks as if it runs for miles. We trudge along this trail for several minutes until we enter a clearing for a campsite labeled Wolf's Den, marked by a tree stump impressed with a carving of a wolf. In the center of a campsite is a fire pit surrounded by rocks to contain the fire. Four thick logs form a square around the fire pit, much like at the infirm, and over this entire campsite hangs a blue plastic-like sheet they call a tarp.

A few people are walking around the campsite, and my eyes lock on the first person in view, and certainly the most eccentric. A girl in a bright-orange fleece and fire-red pants, with knotted, dirty hair in dreadlocks with a feather woven in, is smiling at my dismayed face. My gaze stretches through a tent to two interesting-looking people who seem to be instructors. They look like new-age, granola-crunching yogis who take their jobs very seriously.

The dreadlocked feather girl nearly jumps off her seat toward me in excitement. "Hi! My name's Lizzie! I'm a Wolf and only back at base camp because I'm graduating soon," she yelps at me enthusiastically.

What's she talking about?

I know what my reaction should be: be ready, open, and non-judgmental, and make these people think that I'm changing into what they believe is "right." Instead, fear and shock take over. This girl seems so happy to see another person her age, but the look of sadness in her eyes is paralyzing, and that sadness is overwhelming. I swallow hard, trying to keep panic from bursting through my chest. She looks dejected, like a forlorn kid in a full-page newspaper ad from a social welfare agency soliciting contributions. This makes my own anxiety worse.

A glance behind my left shoulder. P is gone.

A faceless voice chirps, "Hi, I'm Damian, and this is Karen, we tend to stay here at base camp to help integrate the new students into the program."

I turn around and see the two instructors. *Base camp? This isn't even it yet? Great.*

Damian says, "Here at Wolf's Den, we go through your basic steps in order for you to be ready to be placed in your group."

"Group?" I don't like this guy's attitude. Way too chirpy for the situation at hand.

"Basic things like pitching your tarp, rules and regulations, bear hangs, getting through meals, just the normal outdoor wilderness stuff."

Getting through meals? What's there to get through? You just eat your food...

"I can see that you may be a little frazzled," he says.

"Why don't you come under our group tarp and relax for a sec."

I follow him under the big blue sheet hanging above the campsite.

"You're just in time for lunch," Damian says. "The top of your pack probably has a medium-size blue bag inside with your food for the week."

I drop to the ground and wriggle out of the monstrous pack and remove a blue bag from the topmost section. Leaning on the pack for back support, I unzip the blue bag and examine its contents. There's a bag of dried fruit, a hot chocolate packet, a little Ziploc bag of brown sugar, a bag of plain dried oats, some tortillas, a chunk of cheese, and some pretzels. None of this looks appetizing or even edible. I choke back another wave of panic. This can't possibly be enough food for a whole week? Can it?

My expression gives me away.

"That's a small-sized food pack for right now since you haven't entered your group or had expos yet." Damian smiles. "That will get you through these next few days here. Today is Tuesday, so you get a tuna packet and a banana." He says this as if it's a birthday cake for a celebration.

"For breakfast we eat oats with dried milk," Karen says. "You can also put some of your dried fruit, hot chocolate, or brown sugar in to help the taste."

I've never even eaten oatmeal. This might suck.

"It may not be what you're used to," Karen says. She's like a female version of Damian, ruled by rules.

"For dinner, we have what we call group food," she continues. "We divvy the amounts in each person's pack so that the weight is distributed properly when we hike. We generally have lentils, rice, couscous; very starchy, hearty meals to keep us going. Those meals we cook over the fire every night after we finish hiking, unpacking, and setting up camp. Don't worry; you'll learn most of this along the way. Just eat and take this all in for right now."

Another swallow against panic as I turn to look at Lizzie, who's already halfway done with her meal. I'm just starting to make my tortilla wrap with raw tuna.

"It's really not that bad here," Lizzie says softly, "You get used to it. The instructors are really nice." Her expression darkens. "The girls are mean, though, sometimes. I've been here for 54 days and I'm still a Wolf. They brought me here because I'm graduating super soon," she spits out in a hurry. "Why are YOU here?" she asks, her head half turned in question.

I'll come to realize that these are the standard questions for every new person: "Why are you here? What did you do to get yourself here? What's your home situation like? What screwed YOU up?" Maybe the kids already here don't want to feel like they're the only bad ones; they want to find out what's wrong with you, too.

I look back at the girl and give her the most honest answer I have. "I don't know."

"Everyone says that," she snaps, unsatisfied.

We eat in silence till lunch is done. I'm eating because I'm hungry, totally empty, not because the food is any good. Although I do like tuna, but apparently that's a treat?

"Time for PT," Karen announces, which she explains means personal time. "We love our acronyms here!" She beams, once again, overly excited. I'm not sure if this over excitement is supposed to try to lighten the mood, or if this is really how these people talk.

I hate her already. Her exaggerated enthusiasm is too much to handle. This instant, my tears start flowing and won't stop for my self-control or swallows anymore. The others notice it, but for them, it's no big deal, just a normal consequence of being integrated into the program. They just say that I'll get used to it, and this is normal, and so on, until you actually believe that this is reality.

It's PT so I try to take a nap in the corner under the tarp, but Karen tells me that I'm not allowed to sleep now, only on allotted time. *Great.* She gives me a blank journal in which I'll be allowed to write—or required to write—I'll find out. But I'll have to sharpen my pencil on a rock. There are no pencil sharpeners here, she explains. "They could be used as knives," she says with a severe expression. "Some kids have had problems with cutting themselves, so we removed any and all potential triggers."

Sleep control, food control, physical control; the only thing they can't control is my thoughts.

I find out that Lizzie has been "moved groups" because she hasn't been getting along with the other girls, and that's why she's still at base camp. A red flag goes up. I'm set on leaving in 28 days and I'm going to focus all my energy on that goal.

It's close to dinnertime when a new boy approaches my spot under the tarp. He's wearing the same obnoxiously colored clothes we all have on. P introduces him, "This is Anthony, another intake."

Anthony smiles at me and the others. "Hey guys," he says. His smile is warm.

"Generally we DO NOT have boys and girls together at all, not even at base camp, but for one night before you and Anthony are off to your groups, we will allow it," Damian interjects.

Anthony sits down near me, looking much more at ease in the woods than I am. He's taking it all very smoothly—everything Damian and Karen are saying, and Lizzie's weird awkwardness too. He seems determined, like me, to pull it together and get through what's to come. The main difference is that Anthony knew ahead of time that he was coming here. He was prepared.

I take to Anthony and feel some comfort in his voice and his stories from Boston. More than anything, I wish my new friend could come with me to my group. If only he could come with me, I wouldn't be alone in the wilderness.

When it's time to go to sleep, Damian and Karen take away all of my belongings except for my journal and things that I can't run away with. Shoes are a big one that they take away because you can't go far without shoes in a forest. We all have separate tents. Karen sort of helps me make mine, and I crawl into my sleeping bag under my own tarp. Lizzie and Anthony make their tents, and Anthony gets some help too because he's new here.

It's dark now and I can hear crickets and other forest sounds. I'm sad, terribly sad, and I can't make myself feel better. This is a type of sadness that I've never felt before. Getting sent away like this is just one example of how my parents make me feel that I've burdened their entire existence ever since I was born. I can't rationalize that I deserve this because of what I've done, which was nothing more than any other kid my age. Crying alone, I'm thinking how much worse the other kids at my school are and how blind my mother is. If she thinks I have a drug problem, she should compare me with them. After all, she's the substance abuse counselor in my high school. She's around my friends all day every day, and has to talk to so many of them because the local cops like to arrest rich kids for a power trip. Once someone at school gets arrested, the case goes directly to my mother, so she can "help" them with their potential addictions.

It's not ironic that a substance abuse counselor has a daughter who experiments with drugs. In fact, it's probably normal. Her profession has no bearing on my choices, and it never has. I've worked my whole life, ever since age six, and always considered myself an adult. But because of her background in psychology, she's tried to diagnose me with everything under the sun since I was in first grade. She started with, "I think you're dyslexic." I'm not. Then, "Well, you must have ADHD; that's the only explanation for your energy." Umm, I was a child. Later, "No, maybe you are bipolar, yes, slightly bipolar with anger issues. Are you sure you don't want to be on medication?"

"Yes, I'm sure, Mom," I always answered.

My mom started her career as a family therapist and later went into the school system. In my opinion, she's not qualified to help addicts because that was never her line of study, which was clinical and family psychology. She didn't know what to do with me when she thought I was on drugs. She panicked—she yelled at me a lot; she accused me of everything. She suspected me of drinking when I wasn't drinking at all; anytime I came home, she'd have me come into the family room so she could smell my breath, and would accuse me of drinking even if I hadn't taken one sip of anything alcoholic.

I believe my mother finds my choices alarming and threatening to her job and her reputation. The decision to send me away for the summer must have been to ensure that she'd have no more trouble with me. She's afraid of publicity. But if some newspaper or TV reporter publicizes accounts of my drug use, it will affect me much more than my parents, because I've been in the public eye as a child actor, and one making a large stream of money at one time—even more than my mother when I was working on Broadway. This probably bred some resentment. A child at age six to eight making nearly one-third more than my mother's salary must have felt a bit humiliating to my mother, who'd been working so hard as a professional for so many years, and had spent so many years in college and graduate programs, and her only daughter lucked into having a talent.

Publicity would be embarrassing for my mother, and that's what she cares about. She has threatened me since freshman year that if I ever do anything wrong in HER school, a school system I've attended since fifth grade, that I'll be pulled out and they'll send me to school in the next town.

Anyway, why would a reporter want to do a story on my drug use, which is little to none? If you pick any other kid in my high school, you'll get a much better drug story.

A mosquito is buzzing near my ear and I curl up inside my sleeping bag. I hope it doesn't bite me because I'm allergic to mosquitoes and will blow up like a balloon. I am wrapped inside a bug net underneath my tarp, and I hope the holes are too small to let ANY bugs in.

Why am I here? I'm sure my mother convinced my father that I'm so unruly that I'll end up like his younger sister Barbra, who died at 32 from liver failure caused by alcohol abuse. My mother makes him think I'm out of control and abusive, with no direction. In fact, they tell me I abuse them all the time.

My father never says much. When his wife who's a therapist told him, "Michael, I think something's really wrong with her," he probably didn't know what to do, so he listened to Mom and did what he thought was right.

My father is a forensic accountant, which means he can get called into court to testify as an expert witness. He goes through people's stuff and makes sure everything is up to par; or a company hires him because they are getting sued or suing somebody, and they need to sort out their assets. He says his specialty is small-business assessment. All of his cases are confidential, and even if he wants to tell me about them, he never does. I know little or nothing about his daily work, and not much about how he was raised, either.

I think that unconsciously my father fears that I'm going to turn out like his sister Barbra if they don't do something. His older sister Sandi didn't turn out well either; her three grown kids are a mess. Her first son, Seth, is obese and awkward. Her second son, Tracey, is in his 30s with five kids, including two sets of twins, boys and girls, and I think two or three mothers for the children. Then there's Sandi's daughter Kimberly, addicted to meth and with two children who have two fathers, the first of whom beat her. One of Kimberly's babies was born addicted to methadone and had to be weaned off before going home.

My father's father died at 90, angry, belligerent, and drunk. And there's one more troubled relative, my older half-brother from my father's side. He weighs more than 300 pounds and is a manager of a Wendy's fast food restaurant, with no social skills. When he was a kid, he was addicted to porn. I act as if my brother doesn't exist. We have virtually no relationship.

Memories are flooding into my brain, as if I've traveled out of one world and into another. My memories of my parents don't include fun events because we don't have them. There was one family trip outside the country when our family doctor, also my dad's client, flew us to his son's wedding in Vienna, Austria when I was sixteen. That was the one and only time I have been outside the U.S. with my family. I personally have been to eight different countries and spent some time living in Paris, France.

Except for our annual ski trip around New Year's, we never take vacations as a family. Until I was in middle school, we would go to a ski lodge in Vermont, where my dad would ski alone, and I'd be put in ski classes, and my mom, who was very heavy at the time, around 245 pounds, didn't do much besides shop around the ski town and hang out in the lodge. When I got older, I did a couple of ski runs with my dad, but mostly he wanted to do more advanced trails on his own, and that was the extent of our togetherness.

About the only wonderful thing was that my parents came to all of my plays and supported my career and loved to see me onstage. They gave me diamond earrings on the opening night of "The Sound of Music." Until those two escorts came to get me in the middle of the night, I never took those earrings out.

I know my dad loves me, but he doesn't show it. The only time I saw him truly afraid for me and run for help was when we were playing in the park when I was a little girl, maybe around five or six. I was flying back and forth on the swings when I flew off and split my chin open on the square pieces of wood marking the boundaries of the playground. There was a lot of blood, and I needed stitches. My dad grabbed me for dear life and ran like a bat out of hell to get me to the emergency room. That was the one time when I felt a genuine concern for my wellbeing. He loved me and he would do anything for me. Thinking about that now makes me feel still worse. I just wish he understood me better. I don't feel he has really ever tried to get to know me.

With my mom, it's different. We're closer. At least I thought we were. We always used to go shopping together; that was her way of bonding with me. We'd go shopping for new makeup every school year, and for first-day outfits, school supplies, and so on. If I liked something, she'd buy it for me. We were at the mall a lot. I love clothes and shopping, and she knew that would make me happy.

But more than shopping, our relationship was based on trust.

Was.

I told my mother everything. I was always open and honest about *everything*, maybe too much. The first time I had sex. The first time I tried alcohol. Who I was dating at the time. The fights I was having with my girlfriends.

She knew everything about me, which is why I am so confused about why she ever thought waking me up in the middle of the night and shipping me off was a good idea, and good for me. It just simply makes no sense.

Day 2

Soaked.

Consciousness strikes me as I flutter open my eyes and start to wiggle my body around in my tight surroundings. My whole right side is soaked, and I'm zipped into a thermal sleeping bag inside a bug net two inches from my face. That is also two inches from my toes and two inches from my sides. Claustrophobia takes over.

Underneath my bug net is something like a yoga mat, not much of a cushion against the hard ground. Underneath that, there's a plastic sheet directly on the ground to prevent rain from seeping in, yet it looks like that did not do its job. Overhead, above the bug net, is an oddly shaped blue tarp that barely covers my body.

I remember being told last night, very specifically, not to leave my tarp area until after the instructors wake everyone up. But I'm all wet. What am I supposed to do? I roll over and look out from under my tarp and see that not only me, but everything else I have is wet, too—everything that the instructors didn't take from me before I went to sleep. Outside the small area covered by my tarp, I mistakenly left my extra clothes. And my books: I have a skills book containing all my meditations, focus exercises, and writings for personal gain; and a notebook explaining the "leave no trace" way of camping, with instructions on how to set up camp a certain distance away from the water flow, and how to relieve myself a certain distance away from campsite.

Well, it rained, and my tarp was not set up so well for a first-timer in these weather conditions. I'll have to get better at that; I make a mental note.

A new feeling comes along with this wet, dewy, shitty, sunny, in-the-middle-of-nowhere, fucking kind of morning. I want to laugh and cry and scream, all at the same time. What a morning. What a feeling. What's making me laugh is the absurdity of it all—trying so hard to pitch the tent right, trying so hard to focus, and in spite of that, waking up sopping wet with crap everywhere; and I'm laughing about the entire situation of shit I've been thrown into; laughing out of amusement and amazement, and about how ridiculous this all is, and how sudden it was; just laughing for no other way to smile. Laughing to maintain my sanity.

Deep breath in, and out, and in, and out. *I'll dry*, I think. *This is what it is.* I can keep it going. Today is only the second day.

Before long, Damian comes by and drops off big, clear plastic sacks of clothes, shoes, and hiking gear that the instructors confiscated from each of us before we went to sleep. He calls out in a stern tone that we have ten minutes to get dressed and be at the campsite with all of our essential belongings for the day.

Ugh, really, this sucks. Good thing I've been up for a while anyway and there's not much stuff with me. I run through a checklist: shoes, fleece, sitting mat, and my food bag, which we'll get once we are all at campsite and can cut it down from the bear hang. And my composition notebook and the pencil that I sharpened on a rock yesterday. That is the most import-ant thing because they make you write down daily goals at breakfast. Your goals determine whether you are allowed to get spices for your dinner meal. If you do not meet your goals for that day, you are not allowed any spice, which makes the plain beans and lentils quite bland. I also have a skills booklet and a notepad for moving up in assignments and transition phases (Turtle, Bear, Wolf, Hawk). Got it. I think. I go sit down at the campsite, the first one there besides the instructors.

"How'd you sleep?" Karen smiles.

"I slept, but when I woke up all of my stuff was wet. So I don't really know what do about that."

Karen doesn't seem shocked or the least bit sympathetic. "The weather wasn't ideal for your first night here, but at least you got it done with. Now you won't ever set up your tent like that again." She shrugs.

"Yeah, I guess I won't." I feel like rolling my eyes at her with an obviously, "Yeah, duh" face, but refrain.

Lizzie and Anthony put their things down in front of their spots. All of our stuff checks out; good thing nothing is missing.

BREAKFAST

We retrieve our food bags from the bear hang in a tree a few hundred yards away, and then sit down for some oats.

This is what I've been dreading.

The instructors tell me quite firmly that I'm required to eat my entire, full cup of oats in the morning in order to pass the required eating standard. These oats are mandatory, whether I like them or not. There's a bag of dried fruit and a hot chocolate pouch, and also some powdered milk to add in as well. How bad can it possibly be? I mix all these dry ingredients together. The concoction doesn't look terrible. I take a second, evaluate, and eat a spoonful.

This dry, gunky, semi-sweetened glop couldn't taste worse. The ten seconds it takes for whatever you swallow to go down your esophagus is a challenge. Feeling the not-so-chewed dried fruit, bits of oats, and powdered milk almost makes me choke. When I look down at my cup and see how much I have left to eat to pass the eating requirement, I don't know if I'll be able to make it.

I try to swallow. The spoonful of glop starts making its way down my throat. I swallow again in the hope that it will go faster. This is not helping. These oats are just not working. A tear starts to swell in my eye from the nausea this is causing me. *Please*, I plead with myself, *just eat the damn cup of oats. Please!*

More tears, more pain, more nearly vomiting.

"Drink some water while eating." Lizzie nudges me. "It makes it easier. Plus, you have to finish a full Nalgene (water bottle) before we start our day anyway. Better to get it over with."

Now I have a water requirement too?

Another spoonful with Lizzie's advice. Gulp, swallow, water, repeat. Gulp, swallow, water, repeat. *Fuck.*

I look over at Anthony, who seems to be having as much trouble eating these oats as I am. It doesn't look as if either of us is going to hold down this food.

"What happens if I don't eat all my oats?" I ask the instructors.

"Well, that's just not an option," Damian states robotically.

"And why is that not an option?"

He talks to me as if I'm stupid for asking such a question. "If you do not fulfill your food requirements, you will not make it out of Turtle phase. And in Turtle, you can't do much of anything to personally grow. You'll be sitting in base camp, with us teaching you how to eat, until you get it right."

That's a shitty answer, I think. What's with the one-cup thing? Everyone is different sizes, and I'm clearly a lot smaller than the four other people around me. I don't need as much food to function.

Tension rolls up my spine, and I straighten up. I shoot a dead look at Damian, who must know that his answer didn't please me. For at least 30 minutes, all through what they refer to as breakfast, I try to rationalize and teach them logic. "I'm small," I tell them, as if they can't see. But they're not having it, and they keep coming back with the same answer, "That's the requirement."

Gulp, swallow, water, repeat. If it kills me, I'm going to make it out in 28 days, that's for damn sure. And this oats crap is not going to hold me back in Bear for all eternity. Anthony is getting through his cup as well, and we look at each other for support. I take one last excruciating swallow. At that moment, both of us wave our cups in front of the instructors to show that all our oats are finished. But as it turns out we are not finished yet.

"Now you can sump your cup!" Karen squeals.

Sump? Anthony and I return her enthusiasm with aggravated smiles.

The catch to eating in the wilderness is that when you're finished with the food inside your cup, you must clean it out with a method called sumping: you pour a little water into the cup and swish around the remnants of the food inside. You might have to use your fingers to rub off excess food into the water mixture, like some disgusting soup. Once everything is cleaned out, you then drink the remnants in the cup.

I must now sump my cup as well, great! This day is getting better.

Lizzie, Anthony, and I sit and talk for a while, sharing our stories, telling each other why we think we're here, where we come from, what our interests are. It appears that talking through our problems is going to be a big trend throughout this wilderness process.

There's only so much you can pick up and remember from other people's stories, when you're still so locked up inside your own head. Yesterday my parents sent me away, and my life, as I knew it, is now over. No one I know is here. No more California, no more prep for UCLA. That hurts the most, because it's about my future and the career I want so badly and have been working for since age seven.

Three more days, and I was going to be boarding a plane for LA to attend the UCLA Musical Theater Conservatory. It's a great program—three weeks of training and rehearsal for a great musical that's going to be performed on the last day, when I'll probably still be stuck here in the woods, "self reflecting." Students in the theater program get training in everything that I love to do—acting, musical performance, and movement techniques. They say it's the training of a lifetime. I can't stop thinking about the summer I was going to have, yet I try to redirect my thoughts because I know that the painful reality is that I will never get to go.

When I got accepted, I hit the ceiling, I was so happy. I had to audition to get in, and there was a lot of competition. They sent me a fat envelope with all my papers, including a typical daily schedule, which I practically memorized. Each day starts with vocal warm-up for half an hour, and then you have dance class. After that, there's acting technique, intensive vocal skills, comedy, improv, and choral rehearsal. Plus meeting the professional faculty and making all the new friends I was going to have.

But I have no time to grieve. My grieving process is simply, get out of here as quickly as possible. Follow all instructions, and LEAVE! I have blinders on, and they're on so that I can get myself out.

The only thing I can hope for right now is that after these

28 days, I'll be able to go home. Home to my friends and my life, and back in enough time to salvage college. Only 27 more days.

Somewhere in the back of my mind I hear P warning me that she's never heard of anyone graduating after the minimum 28 days. Well, there's always a first. I've always been different.

———

From the outer end of the campsite, P and a woman with a hiking pack are approaching. I haven't seen P since she left Anthony here, and I just assumed I'd never see her again. They're walking at a brisk pace toward the group with an expression I can't read. Maybe Lizzie is leaving finally? Or are they here to take Anthony or me somewhere else shitty? To our groups maybe?

"This is Amanda," P tells the instructors. "She's here to take Marissa to her group."

Finally, I'm going to leave base camp, which is getting boring and aggravating. At least in my group I'll be with other girls to talk to and get to know. I pack up all my wet gear, wave goodbye to Lizzie and Anthony, and walk away with P and Amanda. I will miss Anthony in the coming days.

We slowly hike past grassy areas to my new group. Group C, I'm told. Up and down little hills, dirt roads, in the same old middle of nowhere. We round the next grass patch and up one smaller hill where I see a group of orange- and red-jump-suited girls. All heads suddenly turn in my direction. Some girls are smiling, some look worried, and others have blank stares, but all seem generally happy to see me, a new person.

I drop my backpack and sit next to a small blonde girl who looks pretty much at ease, given the surroundings.

"Hey! I'm Caroline. What's your name?" She's smiling.

"Marissa."

"I'm excited we finally get a new girl in the group," she says. "It's been a while. How was base camp?"

"Umm, not so great," I answer. "I got all my stuff wet the first night because of the rain. There was one nice boy there, Anthony. And a girl named Lizzie." This is a simplified version of base camp, good enough for now.

"Ohhh, Lizzie, I wondered where she went," Caroline says. "She got kicked out of our group because she couldn't work with us properly, so they took her by herself because she's been here for such a long time."

"They separated her from the group because you all didn't get along?" That seems awkward.

"Yeah, I guess that's why. She just didn't fit in." Caroline shrugs. She's playing with a rock.

Amanda comes at me from behind. "Let's get your tarp set up," she says. "This way you can learn all your knots right so it won't be hard on expo."

"Expo?" I ask.

"When we take you off the grounds to a separate location to go hiking for a few days," Amanda explains. "We go off grounds for three or four days, come back for a couple days, and then back out on our next expo."

These words stop me dead: off grounds for three or four days of hiking and camping and eating oats, all of which I'm not sure I'll live through. I wonder what would happen if I accidentally broke a leg? This is a serious possibility while out in the woods. Would my parents think that this was too dangerous and come to take me home? Maybe. Maybe after my first letter to them, they'll understand that this just is not the place for me.

Amanda is already a small distance ahead when she calls back, "Are you coming?"

Back to reality. *Amanda is talking to me. Focus*, I tell myself. I follow after her with my pack in hand.

"We have to make our tarps at least 50 to 100 feet away from our campsites, just to be safe from animals and fires and such." Amanda is striding comfortably to where everyone's tarps are set up fairly close to one another.

"When we're still on the grounds, we have smaller spaces to work with, so we must set up close to one another. But once we're on expo, we'll have plenty more spaces to choose from and spread out our tarps. Make sure you pick an area that's on flat ground. No sunken-in spaces. That would only get you wet when the rain comes and collects right where you're sleeping. And try to stay away from hills and slopes; they are just difficult to sleep on. I'll set up your tarp once for you, and then take it down so you can practice."

Physical skills aren't that hard for me to learn. I watch Amanda closely so I can copycat exactly what she's doing. This part of wilderness, at least, is effortless.

It's a pretty lax day around the campsite with the girls. I'm only a Turtle, so I can't do much with myself besides talk, write, and start my first letter home to my parents. Part of the requirements is to write one full page every day in this journal they gave us. Which just seems like another tactic to manipulate and control us. If we're to write our feelings every day, and then they read it to check off that we did it, doesn't that mean that they can see what we're writing and what we're thinking? It turns from personal to public in one second. This is not a good feeling, and it makes me not want to write anything, to be honest. But I do it anyway, because no matter what, I will leave here in 28 days.

I feel like I'm a prisoner every day, and I've been here for only two long days. This is an entire conditioning system for kids. I don't get the impression that anyone in the program even *likes* kids. These instructors are just granola-crunchers who need jobs as counselors and have a clean record and can handle camping.

Over dinner, I find out that Caroline, the first girl I met, is a 14-year-old alcoholic, now in the wilderness for her 25th day. She's nowhere near graduation or going home. There's no way I can let myself turn into one of these girls.

The thoughts just keep repeating... *28 days, and I'm out of here.*

Pain checks me back into reality and out of my thoughts. I look down at my hand now, burning and itching. The skin around the topside of my thumb and surrounding my knuckles is swollen. One small round circle with a speck at the center seems to be the source of this pain. Slowly clamping my hand hard, I walk across camp over to Amanda.

"Hey Amanda, umm, I think I have a mosquito bite. Is there anything I can do about it? Any anti-itching lotion or something?"

Twisting her crooked smile at me and examining my hand, Amanda sighs. "Well, the thing is that we don't have any medicine to give you unless authorized by the doctor that you saw your first day here. It's just bug session here. So I'm sure it will go down and you'll be fine tomorrow." She's lost interest in my hand already. "Are you going over your growth book to see what you need to be ready for to become a Bear?"

I smile back halfheartedly. "Yup, I'm reading everything thoroughly. Yeah, I'm sure my hand is no big deal." I finish with a deep breath and another fake smile, and off I go, back to my spot on the dirt across camp. Huh, no help.

By the end of Day 2, I'm told that all the girls in my group have reported that I use "big words." This will prove to be my fundamental problem for the rest of my time at wilderness. Super, already a problem that's not my fault. How else can I express myself?

I don't know what these girls are thinking. They're young, all of them, most of them younger than my age, 17, and all of them are angry. They don't want to be here. They're trying to blame anyone for anything, or to cause drama, so they don't have to think about their own problems. By "big words," they mean too advanced for them to understand. I really want to respond, "Sorry that I'm educated." Or maybe they think that I'm trying to undermine their intelligence, or to show that I think I'm better than they are. No matter what, I can't end up like Lizzie, here indefinitely with no end point, all because the group doesn't think I fit in.

Adjusting to the people is going to be harder than surviving in the wilderness.

Day 3

I've become a Bear!

And I accomplish most of my "soft skills" in only a few hours. I'm determined. The writing assignments are a breeze.

Soft skills: all written assignments for personal growth; e.g., writing down a timeline of my past, or writing a page on a ten-minute meditation. A personal inventory of my life; a leadership exercise on who I thought was the most influential person in my life. Oh, and you can't forget my "I feel" statements:

Example: I feel _____ about _____. I imagine I feel this way because _____. In the future I hope this feeling will _____.

Not only do we have to write five of these in our journals every day, but we actually have to express two "I feels" out loud each day. This makes you feel like an idiot, considering that you have to follow the exact "I feel" format every time you state one. If you don't, then you're stuck repeating it until you get it right.

Quick glance at my hand. Shit! This swelling is huge. Just touching the area around my bug bite turns the color of my hand from white to red in each spot I press. The heat emanating from my hand feels like a fever, and it's not going away; it's getting worse. The skin around the area is becoming really stiff.

Benadryl is clearly needed now.

Day 4

First day of expo.

"Make sure you fill up your Nalgenes with water from the spigot," one of the instructors says. "Once we're out in the woods, we'll have to use down-flowing water from streams."

All five of us slowly drag our feet to the spout—Caroline, Lindsay, Christine, Molly, and me. They've all been here for a fair amount of time, Molly the least, for 17 days. We're certainly a sight to see, everyone dressed in bright-red reflecting pants and orange long-sleeved shirts. We're walking so close together that you can almost see the figurative balls and chains connecting us so that we won't run, but only if you look hard enough and squint.

No one has told me much about expo except that it's a lot of hiking. And also that it's impossible to make it out of here in 28 days. Only one person ever got out in 28, I was informed very quickly once I declared my goal, and apparently that was a boy. *Whatever, girls are just as good as boys!* I think flippantly, wishing everyone else would agree.

They say that the first couple of days of hiking with your pack are the worst. Seems logical. I'm a five-foot, 95-pound girl from New Jersey who relies on her car to carry her from spot to spot. I'm a cheerleader and good at sports, but the thought of walking anywhere for a long distance is definitely out of the question, and absolutely not with this much weight on my back.

My current backpack, I'm estimating, must weigh around 45 to 50 pounds. With all of my stuff, plus extra weight from the group's things, my pack is ridiculously oversized for me. The group gear includes lots of items distributed among us, such as group dinner food, pots and pans for cooking, and the group tarp, which is comically heavy because of the amount of fabric required for such a large tarp. There's also the water pump, and ropes for tying the group tent, and other ropes for setting up the bear hang.

Molly is lingering at the back of the water line, deliberately excluding herself from everyone else, so I stay behind and wait for her. I'm new here, but I can already sense that none of the other girls like her very much. She doesn't look like a heroin addict or a druggie; she's actually a bit overweight. *I wonder why she's here.* She's pale with light-blonde, frizzy hair framing a round face, her eyes always sunken in. Shyer than the others, she seems vulnerable and looks harmless and sad. If Molly is at fault for anything, it's her social awkwardness and lack of self-esteem.

I want to be Molly's friend because she needs one; I can feel it whether she says it or not. No one knows how to talk to her or handle her because she's so deeply depressed. No one has the patience or energy to help her gain self-confidence, because they are so focused on themselves, which is what the program tells you to do. But if someone just paid attention to her, she'd be able to hike with the group and become a good member and also a leader, when it's her turn. I have all the patience in the world right now. I don't think there's so much wrong with me, so I decide right now that I'm going to help everyone else. Should look good for me as well as help me grow through others. I feel Molly's pain and I'm sure it's throwing everyone else off as well. I'm going to help minimize her pain for her sake and everyone else's.

I nudge her. "What's up, Mol? How ya feelin' about this hike?"

Her eyes dart away from the rock she's kicking. "Eh, well I don't know. I'm not really good at hiking." She's not looking me in the eye. "What about you? It's your first expo."

"Yeah, I'm sure I'll be fine," I lie. "I've never hiked before. I'm not sure what to expect."

"I don't know where we're going this time, but some hikes are easier than others," Molly says. "Depends on whether there's a trail or if we're bushwhacking straight through the trees with a compass."

"Bushwhacking?"

"Yeah, but don't worry about that right now," she says. "Looks like everyone's done. Let's go. Time for expo." A wide sarcastic smile crosses her face. We both laugh a little, and now we're off, traveling to the trailhead, or wherever, by car.

Inside the blacked-out suburban, I'm paying close attention to the roads we're taking to the site, just in case I decide to make a run for it. I wonder if anyone ever does? Bad thought, would never do it, but if I could, I might...

As much as I want to succeed and get out of here fast, my distrust for everyone here isn't going away. So many "what ifs"—*What if I run? What if I accidentally break a bone? What if I refuse to eat my disgusting oats?*

The scenery distracts me from my errant thoughts. Lush green trees fly past the windows as we drive, a solid block of green for 20 minutes. Roads are short, narrow, and intertwined, and most are unpaved once we're off the main streets and highways. The dirt on the smaller roads is clouding the windows with brown dust particles, and the potholes are so deep that the suburban drops heavily into each one, making for a rocky ride, foreshadowing what the expo is going to be like. We're out in the middle of bumblefuck. I never thought it possible I'd end up like this.

The car stops in front of a wooden gate marking a hiking path. Trees bordering the dirt road are so tall that they block out the sun. It looks like my first roadway through the nine levels of Hell.

All of us delinquents file out of the suburban and wait for our next instructions. Our hiking packs are unloaded from the trunk and strewn out on the dirt road for us to wrestle on. The other girls are throwing their packs around their backs with no problem at all, except for Molly, who asks me for a hand. It isn't easy to carelessly swing a 50-pound pack onto your back like it's no big deal.

I eye my pack, trying to think of the best way to go about this. If I stand with one leg in front of the other and grab one of the straps, maybe I can get enough leverage to lift and swing the whole thing around with one strong-enough tug.

OK, I'm gonna go for it.

Bracing myself with my legs firmly planted on the ground, I reach for the strap, count to three, and yank it as hard as I can. The bag lifts about a foot off the ground, only to pull me crashing back down in the dirt with it.

Well, this is not as easy as it looks. "Molly, can you help me please?" I call to her with a defeated smile.

She scurries over, helps me with my pack, and then all of us are off down the trail, single file like elementary school children.

A few minutes into the hike, I discover that June is mosquito season in the Adirondacks, and the bugs get so bad that the instructors give us all a lesson on how to use our bug masks, which are green nets that you put on over your head so the bugs can't get through. Apparently you can also drink water through your net.

Not even 30 minutes into walking, I start to hyperventilate because of the obesity of this pack that's half my body weight. No one is very happy with me when I want to keep taking so many breaks. They're all good at hiking except for Molly, who takes some heat off of me for my horrible hiking; she's almost as bad as I am. She starts to cry once during one of our three-minute breaks, and she's complaining the rest of the time as well. The others are a bit bothered by the fact that I need to stop so much and that I'm in pain. I'm killing their momentum, they say. They just keep yelling that it's easier if you push through it, and that it takes more energy to talk than to walk. It only gets easier with experience. They just want to get to camp before sundown. I don't blame them.

It doesn't feel like it's going to get any easier.

The counselors aren't saying much, but they encourage us to keep going. One of them says, "You should be thankful that we're on a trail and not bushwhacking with a compass." *Thank you, makes me feel great.* I think to myself.

One instructor is in the front leading, one in the back following, and one in the middle to make sure everything is going OK. They're very trusting. Being surrounded like this makes the notion of running away less appealing.

Trying to follow their advice, I trudge on, pushing my body to its brink.

Walking slowly, I feel something warm hit my hand. Another drip, then another. Is it raining? Then I feel the warm liquid drip down onto my lips. I lick my lip. The taste of blood hits my tongue and I start to get nervous. I haven't had a nosebleed in years. And now I get one? Awesome. This is a bit bothersome. I have no idea why this is happening. Maybe it's the altitude? I walk over to the instructors, hands covered in blood.

"Umm, I think something's wrong." I look over at the instructors, who immediately respond by running over with some gauze to try to stop the bleeding, telling me to put my head back to slow down the bleeding.

I can hear the girls gossiping to each other, "Oh, she must have done cocaine before she got here. Too much blow probably wasn't good for her, she must have lied to us; she must be a serious drug addict."

Gauze in hand, I turn my head and firmly tell them, "I did not do cocaine to make my nose bleed, thank you. I'm not used to the altitude. Any other questions, girls?"

This I am not in the mood for.

LUNCHTIME

Our group emerges from the densely wooded path into a sunlit, open space with a stream. The trail makes a little walkway over the stream and then leads away into the woods, but the open space and running water are beautiful. This clearing looks and feels alive, which is a change from what I've been going through. Everything else besides nature feels dark, and now finally we see sunlight.

One of the instructors, Tim, is standing by the stream waving his empty water bottle over his head. "Did everyone finish their first Nalgene?" he asks. It's part of the drinking requirement to have one bottle finished by lunchtime.

Everyone calls out "last sips" to prove we're not lying about drinking our water and spilling it out or something, and we gulp down the last bit. We all walk over to the stream and watch Tim as he pulls out his small black water filter.

"We always get water from down-flowing streams, and we use a filter," he explains.

The filter has a sphere at one end with slits cut out, which is connected to a black hose that goes to a pump. You put the sphere in the water and pump the water from the stream into your Nalgene to make sure you don't drink any extra glop from the water. This is a time-consuming process, but we aren't getting any water if we don't do it, and it is taking time away from hiking at the moment. After all the Nalgenes are filled up, Tim drops two iodine tablets into each to purge the water of any toxins so we don't get poisoned.

At last I get to sit down and make myself comfortable while I eat. I'm leaning against a big rock in the shade. Starving, I pull out my food bag and push through to the tortillas, pretzels, and cheese. These are the only items that I like. Nobody gets a choice of food over here. I'm not fond of raisins, but I guess they'll be good fillers if I'm still hungry. There's also an enormous bag of dried fruit. I roll up some cheese in a tortilla and take a bite. *Yum.* There's a tub of peanut butter, which I don't like either, but I figure that since it's a whole tub full, that's supposed to be our main source of protein. I'd deal with that later. Right now, I just want to sit and relax, and enjoy the sun, free of hiking for a minute.

TWENTY SHORT MINUTES LATER

"Pack up girls, we gotta get going."

We all put away our food, pack up our bags, lurch our packs back on, and assemble into the same single-file line as before.

The next two hours of the hike are pretty OK. Knowing in advance that it's going to suck, I just walk a bit slower or ask for a break if I need one, instead of outwardly complaining. The instructors are pretty good about giving us five-minute rest periods. But we're not allowed to take off our packs, just lean against something, or it takes away the drive. My back and shoulders are so sore that I can't feel them anymore.

We get to the last leg of the hike, which looks like it's going to get harder. Although, straight ahead, we glimpse a lake, right out in the middle of the forest. Seeing a lake makes everything feel less closed-in on the path. It's like that bit of sun that the stream provided at our lunch spot. Just as we're about to turn onto a smaller path to the left, Tim stops us and says we can walk down to the lake for five minutes. All the girls run down. I hit the ground like a turtle with a pack for a shell and close my eyes. I need a nap.

Deep breaths and motivational thoughts. *I can get through hiking.*

Too soon, Mike, another instructor, yells, "Everybody, let's go!"

Back in formation, the eight of us proceed along a smooth road, its dirt packed down by a tractor to make the ground flat so trucks can get to the campground nearby. The road ends and merges into a trail, but we bear off the trail and head into the woods to make a camp. We're not allowed to use the common lean-tos set up for campers because the instructors never want us to interact with outside people while we're in the program. So instead of hiking to an established campsite, we head deep into the woods with a compass to get us out in the morning. Off trail, the ground is uneven, and we're surrounded by shrubbery and trees. The instructor at the head of the line keeps peering at his compass to make sure we're headed in the right direction.

Now the hike turns into a cloud of mosquitoes, mushy ground, and tangles of branches to shove through. Suddenly I walk right into the back of Molly, who has stopped walking. Swirling around with a big smile, she announces, "We're here!"

Finally! Our campsite. Tim drops his pack on the ground and sits down. We all mimic him like puppets. It's finally OK to sit down and take a long, well-deserved breath. This has been a long, grueling first hike.

Our hiking is done, yes, but the rest of the night is ahead of us.

"Spread out and find a spot to pitch your tent, girls. You have ten minutes to find a spot before we start our first dinner call," one of the instructors calls.

I ask Molly, "What's 'dinner call'?"

"We have a certain amount of time to pitch the group tarp and set up our camp," she explains. "They time us, and we accumulate points with each consecutive call we get in a row. If we miss one, it goes back to zero." She frowns. "Try to hurry up so you can have all your calls in a row. You need a certain number of calls that the group makes on time before you're allowed to transition phases. Even if you're ready to move to Hawk and all your personal hard and soft skills are complete, if you don't have the certain number of calls in a row, you can't transition. So move fast!"

The campsite looks intimidating—super hilly, with little flat ground to make a tent. The thing with making a tent is that you need to tie your main line between two trees about six feet apart. With a shortage of flat ground to begin with, it's hard to find the trees you need in an area that's not on a slope or in a valley. If you make your tent in a valley and it rains, the rain collects right where you and your stuff are. On a slope, it's a little easier, just bumpy and uncomfortable for sleeping.

I watch to see where the rest of the group is spreading out. Following Molly, who makes her way past the other tents, I pick a spot close to her that seems satisfactory for one night.

Some distance away, the instructors pick a place on a small hill for our group tarp. Trees are everywhere, with tall grass, dark bushes, and downed trees on the ground. Everything looks like it did in that movie "Twilight," with mosses and ferns and a wet dewiness that still hasn't dried up from the morning.

Oh, no, not again. A warm, thick liquid is dripping out of my nose. I touch a finger to the drip and wipe it away. Pulling my hand back, I see blood covering my fingers.

All of a sudden my head gets heavy. The forest turns from green to red and yellow, my eyes shut, and I collapse.

———

In the morning, we burn everything up according to the "leave no trace" rule of camping. We dirt the fire pit to prevent forest fires, and we break down the entire camp, grabbing *everything*, nothing left behind. The next night, we'll do it all over again in a new, undisclosed location where we'll hike in the middle of nowhere. During an expo, we'll move to these makeshift campsites as many as four times, if that's the schedule the instructors have set up.

Expos are crazy because we're never at a formal campsite. We never go back to "property," which is what they call the campgrounds owned by the program. Instead, we hike off the beaten path made for hikers and practically hide ourselves, creating our own campsite in the middle of nowhere. Out in the woods, we just squat and pitch a tent and set up a fire pit. Then we all sit under the group tent as we cook our dinner, eat, hang our food, maybe have some personal time, and then go to sleep.

It's been only four days, and I'm so far from civilization that it's like I never lived my other life. There's no past, no future; it's all just the *now* of this moment.

Day 5

As I wake up this morning, my whole body feels sore. I open my eyes, confused about where I am, fantasizing that it was all a dream, and that now I'm lying comfortably in my bed. Adjusting my back against the hard ground, I roll over on my side and feel the rough and rocky terrain under my flesh, making me aware of exactly where I am, and depressing me further about my current state.

Looking around at the other tents, I notice that I'm the first person up. My hand feels tight as I reach for my journal and pencil right inside my tent. There's a hot, semi-hard, swollen layer covering my entire hand.

Fuck. I hate having to take Benadryl. It just makes me tired. But I'm severely allergic to mosquito bites and will barely be able to use my hand if I don't take the antihistamine and just hike through the side effects of drowsiness. Hopefully the hike will be moderate today, and we'll have time to work on our soft skills.

We have different program lessons to complete in our growth book in order to transition between phases, such as personal interviews with each of our peers, and interviews with our instructors. During these interviews, we ask the other person a series of questions about ourselves, requesting their honest feedback. Each question comes with pros and cons. This assignment is supposed to make us reflect on what others think of us, and to see ourselves from someone else's perspective.

Another program lesson concerns leadership. Our growth book asks questions such as: "When you hear the word 'leadership,' what comes to your mind?"

And: "State five phrases you think define a leader."

And: "Who do you think is the greatest leader of all time, and why?"

Another: "What makes you a leader?"

Also: "What is the most important part of being a leader?"

Also: "With this assignment, please include some drawings representing what it means to be a leader."

And last, but NOT least: "What could you do to change yourself, to become a better leader here at ALE?"

If you didn't notice, the last question ties the others to a therapeutic evaluation of ourselves. The point is to make us tie in what we believe about leadership, and who we think was the greatest leader, to what we wrote down for answers. They're trying to make us want to emulate those people and answers.

What an assignment. I know the answers they're looking for already. How can you not see where these questions are going? It's degradingly simple and repetitious, like some kind of catechism of wilderness group thinking.

These exercises remind me of going through worksheets you'd get in class when a substitute teacher showed up with no lesson plan, so everyone just sat there being forced to do meaningless bullshit busywork. Except that out here, in the woods, this dumb busywork is a major factor in what they consider your growth in the program.

Well, I'm eager to get these busywork program lessons done today. And before expo is over, I'm going to write a

letter to my parents to give to Cara, my ALE therapist. I'm
not sure my parents know exactly what they signed me up for.
I miss home. I miss my friends, and my car, and my freedom.
You know, I'm supposed to leave for California tomorrow to
go to UCLA for their musical theater program.

My plan was to do my best there and impress the professors and make connections. Then in the fall when I apply
for college admission, those professors would have remem-
bered me, and I would have had a better chance of getting
accepted. Maybe they would have written recommendations
for me. Going to college in LA has always been my dream. As
I lie here now on this hard ground, I see it all slipping away
because of a decision that was taken from me. A choice and
decision about my future that were only mine to make, and
not my parents'.

––––––

My first working memory of acting was my first equity
production of "The Sound of Music" at Montclair State University in New Jersey. I was six years old, in a wooden dance
room with other child performers. The wood was dark, and
the room was very wide and long, with a piano near the front
by the door and floor-to-ceiling mirrors all along both sides.
We were being taught blocking for one of the scenes. Blocking
is how actors are positioned on a stage and exactly how they
have to move around to be compatible with dramatic effects
and lighting and sight lines for the audience. All of the kids
in the show were running around and dancing and singing
our lines to the beautiful song "My Favorite Things," in the
gorgeous harmonies they taught us.

Flash forward a year and half. I'm seven, going on eight,
and in the Broadway production of "The Sound of Music"
at the Martin Beck Theatre on 45th Street, right in the heart
of the New York City theater district. Now it's called Al

Hirschfeld Theatre in honor of the famous Broadway cari-
caturist.

I'm being pulled out of one of my costumes by a stage-
hand on stage right, thrown into another dress, and pushed
back out onstage behind some fake hedges, waiting for my
cue to walk on with the rest of the Von Trapp Family and
be introduced to Maria, our governess. Captain Von Trapp's
family has seven children: Liesl, Friedrich, Brigitta, Kurt,
Louisa, Marta, and Gretl.

When you're behind the fake hedges center stage and
can't see any of the audience members; the stage is dark. The
minute you walk past the opening and onto the stage, the
lights hit you. If you look out to the audience then, you're
blinded, but are aware of how vast it is. Nearly 1300 seats are
in the theater, all of them occupied. If you look up, you can
see two levels of balcony seats filled as well.

What you never forget is the energy—the sense that thousands of people are looking up at the stage with excited eyes,
enjoying every minute of the play, and you can feel it. There
is no doubt about that. Actors get addicted to performing
because of that feeling, because of the people sitting there and
watching you, loving what you're doing onstage, who even
paid to be there to watch you, getting drawn into the story
that you're a part of.

As a child, I wouldn't have given up acting for anything.
I'll admit that I have many flaws because of it, like some slight
elitism, maybe some narcissism about certain things. I'm only
17, but I feel older because of my acting career. In fact, I've
felt mature ever since I was eight years old. I'm a couple of
years older than the other kids in this wilderness program, but
I actually feel much older than they are, and that's because
I've been an adult for much longer than I've been a child. I
have worked. Maybe not hourly jobs, not mopping floors or

serving food or washing dishes, but I worked, and have been working for a long time now.

Feeling older is the only downside of the experience. (When I get older, I'll tell people I'm tired. Like I've been working for a hundred years.) I lost a lot of childhood memories, and I wasn't able to interact with kids my age very well. I hung out with older kids a lot because it was easier to relate. But if it weren't for my career, who would I be now? I'm stuck out here in the woods, but only for a few more weeks. I still have so much drive and ambition, because in my heart I know that I have talents to share. Something to share...

Sometimes people ask me what I liked best about being a child performer, but actually it's *not* about being a child performer. I still am a performer, and I love to perform because it touches people. In some way, I affect people. Through my voice in singing, or through acting in a play, or in writing this memoir, I evoke feelings in people; I reach them, and I love to see that.

I did commercials, too, and they were easy money. All of my earnings went into my own bank account, locked up in Fidelity stocks. The shoots for commercials were three days max, with a lot of what I call "Hurry up and wait." You do the same thing, say the same lines, over and over and over again, until the client is happy. But I loved it. It didn't matter that the work day was tedious, because two months later I'd be smiling back at myself on TV, and that made it a very cool and rewarding experience.

While growing up, I was aware of the enormous amount of competition among multitudes of little girls who wanted to be in "The Sound of Music" and "A Christmas Carol"— or whose parents wanted them to be. Thousands of head-shots got sent out, and thousands of children were heard and watched, and then called back, and then called back again. The callback process was like a dwindling down of the crop.

For the Broadway production of "The Sound of Music," my manager Shirley Grant sent me to a closed audition, and I managed to get myself a callback. I was thrilled!

For "A Christmas Carol," my agent told me she couldn't get me an audition, so I went on an open call. An open call is when *anybody* can walk in and audition. The sight of all these kids waiting is like a scene from "American Idol." But there was Equity preferential treatment, meaning that kids who had experience and were part of the union were bumped up from possibly spot number 3,000 to spot number 234 or so. I booked "A Christmas Carol" that way, from an open call, even when my manager said I couldn't get in to see them. And I was very proud.

I was always booked for my talent in singing and acting, and I was lucky to be able to do those things without much training. My mom forced dance on me, and I did some of that. I was on the team for gymnastics too. I never took an acting class, but took vocal lessons from age six. Nerves or stage fright never affected me as a child, only when I got older and learned what fear was.

For "A Christmas Carol," I stood out over kids who came from Michigan and other far-off states to audition. They weren't booking me for "my look." For "The Sound of Music," I was an understudy for Gretl, the youngest girl, and Marta, the second youngest. My parents say that I sang better than the other two girls, but I was brunette and all the Von Trapps were blond. My height was between the youngest and second youngest girls, so I really don't know why they booked me. I was probably a strong singer, and I could fit both parts if need be.

Being in these shows was a big deal. An enormous deal. I loved every minute of it.

My engagement with "The Sound of Music" ran for nine months, and it was three or four months for "A Christmas Carol." In both shows, I played principal characters, meaning speaking and singing characters with a purpose, not just part of the ensemble. In "A Christmas Carol" I was Grace Smythe, the main actor. She sings a song to Scrooge to make him realize that his morals have not been so nice.

While the shows were running, I worked every day. For "The Sound of Music," there were three months of rehearsal for blocking and such because this was the original revival of the show, and these details needed to be worked out. The day was 10 to 12 hours long, whatever child labor law allowed, and during this time I was schooled on location by tutors from an education company provided by the show.

When the productions started, I went to regular school in the morning and to the show at night. I got home by 12:30 a.m. and woke up at 7:00 a.m. to do it all over again. On Wednesdays I had to skip school because of matinee shows, and on Mondays I had the day off. For "A Christmas Carol," I was on-location educated for the run of the show pretty much, until after rehearsal season, and then I went to school in the morning and the show at night, or had to miss certain days of school, or leave school early. I remember that the school made special accommodations for me. My grades never suffered, but I know that some of my schoolmates were jealous.

Luckily, my parents were never pushy stage parents. They always prided themselves on "not being those people." We ran across plenty of stage parents, but mine were just supportive.

I feel that having a career at such a young age gave me the edge over normal children in dealing with adults and in so much more: I learned to memorize lines and songs, to manage my time, and to carry myself with confidence. It made adults mad when I spoke back with authority in my voice.

But I had trouble with kids in elementary school. Kids

were jealous because I got to "go sing on Broadway," as they called it, and they made fun of me, starting in fifth grade when I was in my second Broadway show, "A Christmas Carol." Lots of young kids want to be Broadway stars or see themselves on TV. Instead of achieving their dreams, I was the one who had a career, and they all had to watch from the sidelines. On top of that, I was getting smarter at a faster pace than they were because I was in the working world with real adults. I saw a lot of what normal kids did as mundane and immature. From fifth to at least eighth grade, my friends hated when I rolled my eyes and said, "That's so immature." They'd tell me I didn't know what I was talking about. I gave up and just kept thinking it internally, and still do sometimes.

Being an actor made me good at selling and good at talking to anyone. As an actor, you have to be able to take on any role. That experience allowed me to take on any role in any conversation with people and give them what they wanted to hear. And I know that skill is going to help me get out of this miserable situation in 28 days.

As I aged into my awkward preteen years, that was an age range where the auditions started to slow down. When you think of TV shows, movies, and other opportunities, there are lots of parts for grade-school girls and high-school girls, but not many for "in-betweeners," except at the Disney Channel. And Disney takes you only if you are non-union at first, meaning not in SAG, the Screen Actors Guild. I was already in SAG, so I couldn't work for Disney. They like to mold their actors.

I think when I hit 14 I got a little chubby, with chubby cheeks, though I was by no means fat. When you're 16, you need a wrangler on set, which means a handler, because you're not legally an adult. So for the teenage parts, the Broadway shows hire adults who are 18 or older but look young enough to play those characters, because there's no liability. I never stopped getting called. I was just in the awkward years and the calls were fewer and farther between.

And then I got sent away.

———

Now I can see some of the others moving inside their tents. One of the instructors is about to start shouting orders to us.

Off to another day.

Day 6

Another typical day. I'm starting to realize how powerless I actually am here. It doesn't matter if I feel sick, or if I'm nervous about my hair falling out, which it has been since I've gotten here, probably from stress and shock. Whatever needs I may think I have are now null and void. No matter what I say, it will not be believed, nor will I be listened to. Doesn't matter how many times my nose bleeds, or even if I faint.

The instructors pretend to listen and care. They spew out therapeutic terms, and they program various lessons that are assigned to them. Yet if you ask any of them about their background, you find that they are no better equipped to deal with troubled adolescents than any other average Joe looking for a job in the Adirondacks. These instructors are just people who like camping or love camping, and who don't mind dealing with difficult kids as an occupational hazard. None of them has a psychology background. I doubt most even finished college.

And these are the people who are preaching about what the world really has in store for us. I can't believe that my mother, the therapist, with a bachelor's as well as a master's from Boston University, sent me to learn about myself from people who live in the Adirondacks and have little or no com-munication with the world outside of the woods.

They note down everything we say. Private conversations among ourselves are prohibited; one of the instructors always has to be within earshot. And we're kept in the dark about any outside events, as well as the date and time. I'm serious. This is so that we "don't worry about anything but the task at hand." Time of day is considered "FI," meaning future infor-mation. Their philosophy is that we don't need a concept of time.

They're just paranoid that we are trying to scheme to all run away, or to take them on at once and escape. What a lia-bility that would be for them.

Ha, they have half our rights signed over to them by our parents, and then all of a sudden one day the seven of us just bolt and disappear. How would they explain *that* to our parents, who just threw 40 thousand dollars or more down the drain?

Oh well, daydreaming.

It's time to start playing the game.

Day 7

The dewy morning mist wets my fingertips as my hand grazes the ground, reaching from my tent toward my journal. Every day, I've been waking up a bit before morning call. If I wake up early enough, I can finish parts of my program that I might not have time for during the day, especially on expo when we hike most of the day and get limited PT (personal time).

PT is a term the counselors made up for what's supposed to be free time. It's just their cynical way of saying, without making it sound awful, that we really don't have any free time at all. We're allowed to do anything we want during PT, except for sleeping. Some of the girls just sit and talk, which is useless. But usually everyone is working on some sort of hard or soft skill to get it done, and PT is the only chance we get to do those things. The program doesn't allocate time for your hard or soft skills, which you have to accomplish if you ever want to get home. It's like giving kids an allowance and telling them they can buy anything they want, but then they have nothing left over after paying for their school lunch and bus fare.

Today is my first day doing morning call out on expo. It's like in the army, I guess; you have to do a whole series of tasks in order, strictly, and on time. Out here in the woods, everything is harder and slower than on base because the terrain isn't easy to deal with. I should get used to this.

Molly is LOD today—Leader of the Day. This might be difficult. If she's self-defeating to begin with, how is she going to motivate a group of angry girls to get anything done efficiently and on time, let alone get through morning call?

What's tricky is that, in order to transition phases; e.g., from Bear to Wolf, or from Wolf to Hawk, you have to complete a certain number of morning and night calls correctly, on time, and in a row. This big challenge can hold you back from transitioning, which requires five in a row— five straight days of being on point and perfect, morning and night, even after long hikes and receiving upsetting letters from parents, and in sync *together*. You can't transition phases unless *everybody* is perfect. Performance is not evaluated on an individual basis. Everyone has to make the calls as a group. The goal is for all the girls to work together as an efficient team, which is not a bad life lesson. Just difficult with a bunch of brats in the woods.

So far, since I've been here, which is seven days now, I've seen us make call all of twice. This means that out of the three days I've been with the group, we've had six opportunities to make call, morning and night, and have fucked that up four times out of six. With these odds, I'll never get to Wolf phase and no one will ever graduate. Today, with Molly as LOD, morning call will be a long shot.

I hear some rustling sounds around camp. The instructors' footsteps are coming closer. One of them shakes my tent and throws in my bag of clothes. Naturally, they can't find a more graceful way to wake us up.

"Five minutes to be up at the group tarp, staaaarting *now!*" one of them yells.

Great, let's get ready for another day. I grab all my stuff as fast as I can, throw on the clothes that were dropped next to me, and sprint to the group tarp, hoping that everyone else makes it there in five.

MORNING CALL

You'd think morning call would be easier than night call. It happens right after breakfast, when we pack up our campsite and our stuff in time to leave for hiking and changing camp-sites.

The instructors set a timer for around 15–20 minutes to complete the call. That sounds very tight, but it's more than enough time to get everything done. Whoever is LOD gets to appoint everyone to a specific job and to assign them what to carry in their pack.

That's cool and all. Except that no one ever wants the job they're assigned. And no one ever wants to carry the items they're assigned. Some of these things are much heavier than others. For instance, no one ever wants to carry the group tarp because it adds an extra 5 to 10 pounds onto someone's pack. And when you're hiking with a 40-pound pack to begin with, that extra weight is painful and it slows you down.

Luckily though, Molly is my friend, and she wouldn't do that to me on my second day of hiking. I already almost had a heart attack within the first ten minutes of yesterday's hike.

For morning call to go successfully, things need to be broken down. Our group tarp has to be disassembled, folded, and stuffed into someone's pack. There's a fire pit used for food and heat in the center of the group tarp. That needs to be stomped out, and wet or damp dirt has to be piled securely on top of it so we don't start a forest fire. We have to take down the bear hang, which is where we hang our food bags after dinner to keep bears and other animals from wandering into our campsite. Our own personal tents and equipment have to be taken down and stored in our packs.

A couple of girls have to go down to the nearest water source to filter the water and fill up all the girls' empty Nalgenes. We're required to gulp down a full bottle of water by the time first call is over, another major annoyance. When you're in such a hurry, you feel like you're drowning yourself with your own bottle of water.

All of the other group materials have to be distributed evenly to all the girls to carry in their packs. Besides the group tarp, this includes group pots, group ropes, group food, and the water purifier.

Before the timer runs out, everyone has to be sitting in a circle where the group tarp used to be, all packed and ready to hike.

AFTER BREAKFAST

Molly assigns both of us to break down the group tarp. She's carrying the pots and I'm carrying the water purifier. Everyone else is OK with their jobs as well.

Ready, set, GO. We all sprint to work.

21 MINUTES LATER . . .

We miss morning call by *one minute*. Rolling my eyes, I take a deep breath.

From the corner of my eye I see Molly silently crying a few feet away. Even though she's the black sheep in the group, I like to help her because I seem to be the only person she's receptive to. The other girls in the group and even the instructors constantly get frustrated with her. She's here, dropped into this shitty situation like the rest of us, yet she doesn't see a future. The light at the end of the 28-day tunnel I see in my eyes, never reaches hers.

Molly wears her depression like a garment. Her cloud of

light-blond, frizzy hair looks as if she doesn't know how to
tie it back. Her cheeks flush rose at a hint of frustration or
failure, and they're puffy, too, making her infrequent smiles
look so wide and innocent that they break your heart. Or at
least mine. Her eyes follow her feet while she's hiking. Eye
contact is almost impossible.

I don't know why the others give her such a hard time.
Maybe it's because the sadness she projects is overpowering
and devastating, and it threatens to envelop those around her.

You know how kids in school have a group mentality
and usually reject a few other kids as outcasts. The victims
sit alone at lunch and don't get picked for teams or invited to
parties. Kids are quick to group themselves according to popularity. I was never accepted by any particular group; I'm a
drifter—I drift between groups. Weaving in and out. I talk to
everyone, popular or not. Even though I've been getting tormented and bullied because of a stupid video, I'm still considered popular but don't have a set group of friends. I keep
many friends from multiple groups and see the significance
of everyone. Because I've been exposed to a world outside the
Tenafly rich-kid bubble, I see the world a bit differently; some
say, with rose-colored glasses.

Helping Molly makes me feel a little better about this
awful experience. I like helping people. It gives me a sense of
self-worth to be able to affect others in a positive way. There is
always a ripple effect. Making one small gesture helping one
person can end up affecting multiple people from that one
original source. We're all connected in some way.

There's got to be a way to reach Molly. I swing my hips at
hers, playfully knocking her off balance a bit. When she sees
that it's me, I finally get a smile.

"What's wrong, Molly?"

"I don't know." She looks down and picks at her finger-
nails. Her eyes glisten because of the sun reflecting her tears.

She takes a deep breath and blurts it all out at once. "I've been here for 26 days now, and I'm still a Bear. No one, including me, thinks I've improved at all. I suck at arts and crafts, and I'm not that good with using my hands to build things for myself. So sparking fires I haven't been able to do, and I can't even conceive of making pieces for my traps. And on top of all this bullshit stuff I need to do to fill the requirements, they say I still haven't 'emotionally grown with my soft skills'."

Full-on streams of tears now. "I'm tired, and I'm hurting, and I'm not improving. I'm sorry I was such a shitty LOD this morning that we missed call. I try; I just don't get it right. I don't wanna do this anymore. I don't wanna be here, I can't." She sits down in the dirt.

I squat down next to her and touch her shoulder. "I believe in you Molly. And I know you can do this." I hold her by her shoulders and stare into her eyes. "I need you to show yourself that you can. I know it's hard, but remember I'm always a few feet away to help you if you want. We all need help sometimes, it's OK. OK?"

My eyebrows rise with the last OK, hoping for a positive response. All this girl needs is affirmation, yet it seems like for her whole life, no one ever gave it to her.

She sniffles. "OK, I'll try."

Slowly, with one arm holding mine, she pulls herself, pack included, off the ground to stand. "I can do this," she says softly.

"Is anything wrong, girls?"

We both turn around to look right into the face of a smiling stranger. "I'm Beth." She gives us her hand to shake. Her hair is pulled back in a braid that sticks out from her baseball cap. Her other hand is holding onto the sides of her backpack, which is much smaller than the rest of ours and appears to have room enough for only one day's worth of food.

This is weird, I think. *Is Beth here for only one day? Are we going back to property?* I look skeptically at her, puzzled about why she's here. I take her hand.

"I'm Marissa, and this is Molly."

Molly shakes her hand too.

"I just got here," Beth says. "I'm a new instructor here to aid you girls in anything you need."

This is all out of place. Even I know this, in only the first week. Molly glances at me in the same confused way that I was staring at Beth. No one moves while we all make silent judgments of each other at first sight.

"Thanks for the offer," I say to Beth, "But we're fine right now. Thanks anyway."

I grab Molly's arm as we head toward the group line to start hiking. Another fake instructor here for an unknown reason I can't handle right now. The group keeps walking off toward another campsite.

This has been by far the most grueling hike yet, and not because we're bushwhacking or going uphill. Actually, the contrary. We're on the same marked-off hikers' trail as on the first day of expo. Except that today we're walking back to where the bus dropped us off.

Since my talk with Molly and Beth's mysterious appearance, no one is in good spirits for today's challenges. You can hear Molly's sniffles from the front of the line, seven people away. We seem to be taking many more breaks than normal, stopping every five minutes to sit down because someone can't go on.

Suddenly Molly stops walking. Sits, starts to cry, and refuses to speak to anyone but me.

Of course the instructors won't let me talk to her. Now Beth is sitting with her a hundred yards away from the group. We all watch and wait, hoping that Molly will get up and continue hiking. Gossiping, we speculate on what will happen if she doesn't get up. Will they make her move by force?

Thirty minutes pass. We're all watching silently.

I'm sick of this. I throw off my pack and storm over to one of the instructors still sitting with us. "Let me talk to her!" I say. "I know what's wrong. She is asking for me. Why won't you let me help her if she is obviously refusing your help? Maybe I can get her to keep hiking with us. Why can't I talk to her?" I plead with them.

"Go sit down, Marissa." The instructors point at the group, coldly, stone-faced. "We have this under control. And unfortunately you cannot help."

I have no choice but to obey them. I sit back down.

Thirty more minutes of Molly not moving.

Beth walks over to us. "You guys are going to keep on hiking and I will stay here with Molly. I will make sure that she is OK. Don't worry about her."

"What?" I shout out. "You're keeping her behind?"

"Yes, but it is for the benefit of the group."

"Is she coming back?" another girl asks.

"I'm not sure," Beth says.

"Is she going to be camping with us tonight?" a different girl calls out.

"I do not know."

Outrage flashes through the group as we all start talking at once, asking "Why?" And "What's going to happen to her? Where will she go?"

Every question ignored.

This is information that they cannot tell us; information they don't want us know.

An instructor orders us, "Group, let's put on our packs and start going. We've lost a lot of time and need to be able to set up camp in daylight."

Queuing up again, I look back at Molly, still crumpled on the ground, shaking and crying.

I call back to her, "You can do it, Molly! Don't give up, and get back to us soon! We need you! I need my friend!"

She looks up from her hands, giving me a sign that at least she heard me.

Then I run after the group.

———

Worrying about Molly, I really hope this isn't the last I'll see of her. She's an outcast around here, and outcasts get bullied. I know that because it happened to me. Kids started making fun of me in fifth grade when I was in my second Broadway show, "A Christmas Carol." I knew they were jealous, but that didn't make it any easier.

During high school I was a fine kid. I did my work and got good grades. I was a cheerleader too, starting in freshman year. That year, I got a great part in the school play because of my background in theater as well. All was looking good.

In November, when the show's run was over, we had a cast party. The cast and crew broke down the set after the last show and smashed all the pieces that we needed to throw out. We destroyed the set with hammers, and then we went to someone's house and got hammered. This was the first party my mother ever let me go to in high school.

It was a Saturday night and Mom agreed to let me sleep at the home of my friend Brooke, a sophomore. But Brooke got drunk at the party and didn't want to go home and face her mother quite yet. I drank some beer but wasn't drunk, just happy and a bit tipsy. It was one of my first encounters with alcohol and I didn't like it much because it made me feel sick and shitty before drunk ever came along.

Two nerdy guys at the party offered us a ride home. They were geeky AV (audiovisual) kids who always carried around video cameras. Documenting everything for fun I guess—memories? Alex was smart, but the other guy was a mildly retarded EMT. Literally, mentally challenged.

Brooke said, "Let's go with these guys."

I agreed, not thinking anything of it; in fact, I was probably smiling and making peace signs and running around because I was a 14-year-old girl having fun at a cast party with all the upperclassmen for the first time ever.

Camera in hand, Alex asked to see my bellybutton ring. Without a care at all, I lifted up my shirt to show him while his video camera whirred.

Daylight came, but we weren't heading anywhere, just driving in circles around the hills of Tenafly. The boys said, "Take off your shirt and show us your boobs, and then we'll drive you home."

I refused. This was a ridiculous request. Bluntly asked, rude, and plain stupid. Annoying.

"Flash us your tits, or we won't drive you home."

I got out of the car and started walking in frustration while they filmed me walking away. They followed me in their two cars, blocking my path. Angry now, I ran and leaped onto the hood of one of their cars, slamming my fist on the hood, hoping to dent it so they'd leave me alone.

"Drive me home," I screamed at them through the window.

The door locks clicked, locking me out of the cars. They drove circles around me for five minutes before finally letting me back in the car as Alex said, "Fine, you don't have to show us your boobs, but bite down his zipper and we'll drive you home." *What?* They wanted me to pull down the other guy's zipper with my teeth. What satisfaction does this give anyone? The kid was wearing those Abercrombie jeans in style at the time, with a string tie that was four inches long.

In my head, I was just aggravated; annoyed that they were

being idiotic boys who wanted to see boobs for the first time. I wasn't so much angry with them. They were like children who didn't know any better than to act like fools. You can only be angry later; and I was. I thought to myself, *Fuck it, I'll do this and then they'll leave me alone. I don't even care if I walk into my house at 6 a.m. My mom will understand.*

I bit the stupid zipper down while the camera whirred, and then they drove me home.

By Monday morning, 1,200 kids from my school had downloaded the video that Alex made about me. He titled the video "Dumb Slut" and put it up on the Internet for everyone to see. Alex cut it so that the image switched right as I lifted my shirt to show him my bellybutton ring, with a caption that popped up after the cut frame, reading "Only for our eyes." Then came shots of me walking and jumping on the car. Another caption read "If she walks so many miles, all the jizz calories will wear off." Then came the shot of me biting the zipper down. In the last shot, I was lying back in the passenger seat, smiling, probably from earlier in the night before this had gone on. The soundtrack consisted of Brooke's sex noises with André 3000's song "Roses" playing in the background. Credits rolled, naming me as the dumb slut and Alex as the editor.

For two entire years following this incident, I walked down the hallways in school, tormented as older girls screamed "Dumb slut!" and various variations as I passed. I was still a virgin, but they didn't care; I was simply the target of their bullying. Someone always has to be the scapegoat, right? Teachers and administrators saw what was going on, but they all sat by and did nothing because the school had no anti-bullying policy and clearly didn't know how to rectify this situation in any way.

My mom is still the substance-abuse counselor at Tenafly High School, and now she also deals with bullying, which is ironic because I got bullied so much. She doesn't tell my story. I think she finds shame and embarrassment in it, which is sad, because that story alone could probably help a lot of young girls in similar situations now. Especially with all this sexting crap going on. Sexting wasn't even a term when I was in high school.

In my junior year, I got a boyfriend of sorts, Mark, who protected me and helped me rebuild my image. He restored my social life because he was very popular and would argue with people on my behalf, explaining that their misperceptions of me were based on a video that was a cruel joke and untrue.

When Ally, the school's mean girl, called me a slut at a party, Mark retorted, "Ally, you've drunk more cum than soda in your life. I wouldn't be calling anyone a slut."

Ally shut up and never bothered me again.

It was with Mark that I started smoking pot. It made me more comfortable with my surroundings and myself. It slowed my already excitable personality down. It was a social thing, too—when people wanted to smoke and I was there, it forced them to spend at least ten minutes with me, during which time so many of them discovered that I wasn't all these awful things they'd thought about me.

Junior year was a breakthrough. I got more apologies than I can count from hundreds of kids in school, all of them regretting that they'd followed the trend of making fun of me and not knowing why. Now that they saw that I was a really nice, cool girl, there was nothing to denounce me for. I made a lot of friends that year who are still with me now.

At the end of my amazing junior year, with everyone coming back to me and apologizing for how they'd mistreated me for the two previous years, I was sent away. I got taken, just as my life was finally starting. Did my parents think I was a bad kid because I started getting invited to house parties for the first time in my life? I was a loser in my freshman and sophomore years, and now I'd gained some popularity, friends, a life, things to do, people who actually liked me. I got ripped from it all and thrown into the woods right before I came into my own.

What Alex did was deplorable. In my opinion, he should have been expelled, but all he got was a five-day suspension for the two and a half years he made me suffer. Bullying is no joke. Kids kill themselves because of bullying, and all educators should be concerned about that.

My parents didn't want to sue the school district because they didn't want the matter in the public eye. They said they didn't want it to affect my career in any way, and they must have been thinking of theirs, too.

While my nightmare was going on, no one helped me or was on my side; all of the bullying was brushed under the rug. And I never cried about it; just walked through the halls knowing that I had truly done nothing wrong and I was a great person, far from the slut that everyone was calling me. I was a virgin who had not done much of anything besides kiss a boy. I didn't care what they thought of me because, in my heart, I knew they were wrong, and I found solace in that knowledge.

Day 8

Everyone is silent at breakfast, glancing around at each other's confused faces, with unspoken questions—Where's Molly? Is she coming back? What's going to happen to her?

The instructors themselves weren't sure how it would turn out yesterday. If Molly had gotten up, we would have continued hiking. The other girls expected her to stop walking and give up. I saw it coming too. I just wish she hadn't stopped.

Last night we got to our campsite well after dark. Making our tents, setting up camp, and getting dinner prepared was practically impossible to do in pitch darkness. Each instructor had a small flashlight. But a tiny stream of light wasn't too helpful.

"We're going back to property today," one of the instructors blurts out. "Yesterday was rough with Molly's departure and setting up camp after dark." She's pacing around the campsite. "We have only 15 minutes for morning call today because our cars are here to take us back." She tells one of the girls, "Lindsay, you're LOD. Time starts now." She clicks her stopwatch.

We all scatter and break down our personal tents. Making call this morning feels good—a new start. Maybe we can hit five days in a row. Property should be easier for making calls.

Walking on the trail to the cars, I look forward to getting back and showering, and enjoying flat ground with a two-day resting period from hiking. I hope.

Behind the metal gates marking the trailhead are the two black suburbans that brought us here. As I drop my pack in the trunk, I catch my reflection in the tinted windows. First glimpse, I don't even recognize myself; I think it's someone else's reflection. My hand goes to my mouth, and now I know it's me. I'm shocked. But I can't show it.

The thing is, you're not allowed to look at yourself while in this program. There are no mirrors, *anywhere*. Body image is a huge issue for a lot of the kids who enter the program, so they remove any type of temptation to judge yourself, look at yourself, or feel anything about your appearance. I can't let the instructors notice that I'm trying to sneak a peek at my newly blown-up face. Walking past the same window, I take one more quick sideways look. Startled, I feel my face, not the smooth skin with invisible pores that I had before. My fingers run over cheeks covered with bumps, some bigger than others, some warmer to the touch, some harder or softer.

My breath is getting short and my face is hot. Quick breaths in and out. I'm close to having a panic attack. I almost collapse at this hideous sight.

Come on, I tell myself, exhaling hard, *Can't I get one break here?* I already felt helpless. This is worse. Mosquito bites are covering the whole surface of my face.

Immediately they start to itch, now that I'm aware of what's going on. The floodgates open and tears start pouring down my cheeks. Turning away from the car, I walk over to Lindsay.

Breathlessly I ask, "What do I look like, Lindsay?"

"Well," she considers, eyes roaming my face. "You don't look the same as you did the first day in our group." Head tilted, she's trying to minimize the damage.

My hands are still clutching at my face, fingers feeling around, and tears streaming down my cheeks. Lindsay can see that her answer isn't helping.

"It's OK, Marissa. They're just bug bites, and maybe some pimples you got because you're not used to this environment," she says. "We all assumed you knew you had them because you were taking Benadryl anyway for your hand."

Caroline comes over. "What's wrong? What happened?"

"My face," I cry.

"Ohhhhh, that." She smirks.

"This isn't funny!" I snap back. "Your face doesn't look like this, now does it?"

"No, it doesn't," she says. "But you're gonna have to get over it because there's nothing anyone, not you either, can do about it." Caroline walks away and stands next to Camille, both of them staring at me.

Defeated, I jump into the car, looking forward to the ride back.

———

Back on property, we set up camp at a much smoother location than in the woods. We still have to walk a bit from the main cabin where the showers are, where the black cars dropped us off. But this is much easier than bushwhacking in mosquito-infested semi-swampland. Property is dry and less lush. Winding through most of the property is a dry dirt road about three cars wide and forever long, with pathways branching off to various campsites for the groups in the program. Instructors radio each other with walkie-talkies to make sure we're on different paths so we won't bump into kids from other groups.

There are six campsites miles apart from each other off the dirt road. At any given time, there are six groups of kids in Adirondack Leadership Expedition facilities: three for girls and three for guys. Guys and girls are separated, and the campsites are too far apart for any of the groups to cross paths. Even if you screamed as loudly as possible, the other kids wouldn't hear you across the distance.

Every time we get back from expo, we're supposed to meet with our therapists. I have never met mine, but I've heard that her name is Cara. I still haven't gotten my impact letter either, though I've heard other people's letters. Some of the girls received theirs while on expo, and they spent the night crying and reading them aloud to us after dinner. I know I'll get mine soon, because I need to read it before meeting with Cara. I wonder what kind of organized, formulaic, psychology-tainted bullshit I'll have to read.

We're having lots of PT today, and I've sparked a few fires with help from Lindsay. She's the nicest girl in the group, and also the oldest, turning eighteen in December. After ALE she's going to an adult rehab facility in Bend, Oregon. She's a recovering drug addict who's done everything under the sun, but she became a junkie only recently, just before she got sent away. She was shooting heroin into her veins for a rush—pulling a bit of blood into the syringe and then shooting the drug into it. And she was snorting speed balls, combining uppers and downers, and doing psychedelics and speed. She has told me stories of drugs I've never heard of before.

Lindsay is tall and skinny with long, stringy brown hair. Her voice sounds jaded and slightly angry, as if she's seen everything in life already. Only in her most vulnerable moments does she sound defeated. I can imagine what she must have looked like while strung out—fingers twitching, eyes darting around the room nervously, all unkempt and dead-looking, nodding out between hits of heroin. She doesn't look much better than that over here; there's just more color in her cheeks without all the drugs she was taking.

I take to Lindsay more than the others because she's the

easiest to talk to. Not that I have a terrific bunch of girls to choose from: Caroline, a fourteen-year-old alcoholic; Camille, a sixteen-year-old druggie; and Christine, a fifteen-year-old sex addict.

Christine is pale as porcelain and has a roly-poly, plump physique. She's passionate about horseback riding and even has a few horses that she's competed with. You'd think that having an interest like that would have kept her sane. But she's here for more than sex. Her parents sent her here for drinking and doing typical drugs and also for failing completely out of school. She seems slightly disturbed and is socially awkward.

Although Christine looks perfectly innocent, she actually lost her virginity at thirteen. Her secret obsession is having sex with black men, sometimes two in one night. She comes from a common small town in middle America, not a wealthy place, where there's not much to do besides drugs and sex. Imagine a mediocre, lower-middle-class town that's a bubble—that's where she calls home.

Around here, the groups fluctuate; I'm told that people come and go. There can be from four to seven girls in the group at one time, and they weave in and out. When some girls leave or graduate, others arrive.

But Molly is still gone. She was just sad, but all the others are angry. They've all found something or someone to blame for everything, and they're angry because of it, angry about their situation and circumstances. They're defiant in their belief that they don't need any help. And they're just as frustrated as I am about being stuck in the woods with no foreseeable endpoint.

At least Lindsay is just a junkie with a cool personality and entertaining stories.

———

After dinner, I get my first impact letter. Where that

term comes from, I don't know; we didn't get an explanation, although I think it's because the letters are meant to be "impactful," that is, meaningful. The instructors expect you to cry, or yell, or curse, or to demonstrate some visible reaction indicating that you don't agree with the letter or you're hurt by it. What I do know is that parents are given a format for the impact letters and they're advised which points to touch on.

Here's the letter, with commentary by me in parentheses. Just before opening my letter, I remember what Anthony warned me about in the car while we weren't supposed to be talking: "Beware of the impact letter," he said. "It's not really from your parents. It's from the therapist here who's manipulating you."

June 21, 2006

Dear Marissa,

    We all know that things were getting very tense and impossible at home for all of us. As parents, we were very uncomfortable with decisions that you made. We felt we needed to take some kind of action, as everything we tried was not working. With information from a number of different sources, we found the Adirondack Leadership Program, and after reading about what it had to offer and speaking to other parents whose kids had gone through the same program, we decided it was our best choice for you. We felt that we were out of options, and because we love you so very much, we needed help to try to get you to make changes. We know this program will help you to do this.

    (Though I'm very young, seventeen years old, only some months away from becoming an adult at eighteen, what changes do you really want to make in me? How much are you trying to change me in your desperate effort to turn me into the child you thought I was going to be?)

As we told you in the letter we sent up with you, our concerns were numerous. For us it was difficult to say or do anything that was parental, because it was your way or the highway. Any rules we set, you negotiated, (interesting choice in words, "negotiated." I never broke the rules, though. Why is it my fault that you're susceptible to negotiation?) to the point where it took so much out of us to fight with you, we sometimes gave in, knowing it was not the best decision. This whole year has been a nightmare, not only at home, but at school as well. Your drug use, as we saw it, was a daily occurrence. In your estimation it was only "weed"; however, you tested positive for cocaine. From a parent's perspective, this was a devastating revelation, even if only an experiment.

(I'm not denying that I tried cocaine with my friends when we all discovered what it was. It did come up on my drug test because I got screwed. I had tried cocaine two days earlier with a friend and happened to get drug-tested shortly after. I was never hiding my experimental days, because I didn't ever plan on these drugs becoming a lifetime habit, as I told my parents so many times. Up until seventeen I hadn't even ever taken a puff of a joint or cigarette. And for one year I wasn't allowed to be a normal kid? Come on. That warrants *this*?)

In addition you felt no problem taking a friend's Concerta prescription on days you decided you needed to focus.

(The only time I ever took Concerta, *once*, was right before the fucking SATs!)

This pattern of using drugs to suit your needs was alarming for us. It was a tremendous shock to see you come up positive for cocaine, when you told us so many times that this wasn't for you. Not only did drug use become an everyday issue, but the life-style that went with it was disturbing as well. You left school in the afternoon and we sometimes didn't see you at home until 9:00 p.m. and often later, (OMG judge and jury, 9:00 p.m., holy shit. What a late-night walker I was.) as you always found good enough excuses for being out, even over our protests.

(Let me say one thing about 9:00 p.m. and good excuses. School ends at 3:30, and I had cheerleading practice until around 7:30-8:00 p.m. Then I'd maybe go to dinner for an hour with my teammates. Mind you, I was doing this at seventeen years old, with a $30,000 car I had paid for myself. After working my ass off on Broadway since age seven, I think a dinner hour alone with my friends was well-deserved.)

All the kids in your group of friends, depending on which group, were getting in trouble over their use of drugs.

(My friends were. Some got pulled over in their cars, and they happened to have pot out and that's what they got nabbed for. A gram of pot. Or underage drinking at the school party.)

Another important concern was your blatant defiance and lack of respect of authority. For us, it was hard to come home to our own house because we couldn't deal with the verbal abuse on a day-to-day basis.

(That's just simply not true. I tried to avoid them as much as possible because no matter what I said or did, I got in trouble for. They were always home, waiting for me to walk in one minute late, ready to start another argument on why I was a troubled youth going downhill.)

At times we didn't want to answer the phone, because it would just provoke another fight. At school, you had to know that things were not good. After three suspensions in one year, all for insubordination,

(1- for parking in the senior parking lot; 2- asking for help from the guidance department for being brutally teased, and when I was denied, I said that one of them needed therapy; 3- I hit a locker because I was upset and someone saw me.)

and two letters home about your possible inability to return,

(Those were the same letters they send home every year because I'm not a resident of Tenafly. I live in the next town over, Cresskill, but my mother is the drug and alcohol counselor at my high school in Tenafly, and they let me go there for free. The Board of Education sends home letters every year, making me write yet another response stating why I want to stay in Tenafly. I don't know why my parents view these as threatening as I'm going into my senior year. When we've received the same letter every year since I was in fifth grade.)

had to clue you in that you had pushed things to the limit. There are better ways to get your point across.

(At this point this whole letter sounds like I'm a monster child from a completely distorted viewpoint.)

Another important concern was about your total lack of any family involvement. Very early on this year, you chose to never come out with us. When Jared and Mary would show up (my half brother from my father's side, 20 years my senior, and his wife), you would leave and I could see the disappointment on Jonathan and Ben's faces (my nephews), even when you couldn't. Mother's Day was a huge disappointment. And maybe we made it easy on you not to participate in the barbecue for Father's Day; however, it was still upsetting and hurtful. You even handed Dad a horrible letter on Father's Day.

(I wrote a letter to my father explaining my emotions and why it was difficult for me to communicate with him. My bad. Didn't realize it was Father's Day when I handed it to him, but nothing in that letter was false, and a communication change really did need to happen. So instead of arguing with my parents as usual, I wrote my feelings down instead.)

Although you may not see his support, he is there for you all the time and is hurt by your rejection. Dad could not even get past the first sentence of your letter because he had been through enough.

(Maybe if he'd read my letter he'd understand how I felt, instead of throwing it away and disregarding my feelings and focusing on his own pain, channeling that, and sending his daughter away.)

As far as Mom, she just feels beat up. She remembers dinners out from past years and how much you shared of your life, especially your stories; and that is all gone.

(Gone because I was scrutinized and chastised for telling her the truth.)

She is embarrassed by your behavior at work toward her.

(My mother and I would get into arguments

and yell at each other in school—in the hallways, in offices, wherever.)

You have cursed at her and talked back to her and yelled at her in her place of work.

(My mother has as dirty of a mouth as anyone else, and uses it against me too. I'm not the only one making off-color remarks. No one at school really hears us yelling at each other. She has a separate office in the senior hallway where you walk in and can close the door, much like a therapist's office, so it's private. She and I yell when people aren't around.)

It is a hard thing to accept from your own child.

You also seemed to have lost interest in things that were so very important to you. Even in the middle of the year you were still going to local concerts, but of late, have given up those friends.

(Sophomore year, I turned into an EMO kid for *one second*. EMO kids have distinctive tastes in music, clothes, and so on. And I helped throw those local firehouse concerts where the kids dress all in black with triple XXXs on their hands for sobriety. They would scream sad lyrics about cutting themselves. I think it's safe to say that that crowd was not going to be where I resided for very long.)

We don't hear you sing much anymore, possibly because you are not home much.

(BINGO).

Cheerleading went by the wayside, basically because of drug use.

(Let's get this one straight. I loved cheerleading. Lived for it! I was on the Varsity competitive squad from the minute I tried out for the team as a freshman. Even when I shattered my heel right before competition season, I sat there every day with crutches during practice and watched the girls, just to be part of the team, waiting for my chance to compete sophomore year. Sophomore year went fine. My skills improved and I was put in more stunts because I'd recovered.

A lot of turbulent things happened to me throughout high school. Like getting framed for smoking pot and kicked off the cheerleading team at the beginning of junior year because the girls were jealous that I was the new really great flyer. I was more athletic and better-coordinated than the others; smaller, lighter, more aerodynamic; and I was a quick learner. My acting experience helped me perform, and I was very enthusiastic about cheerleading.

But the current flyers on the squad who were already doing so-called "cool high-profile stunts" saw me as a threat. They were always obnoxious and never nice to me, and they tormented me the entire time I was on the team.

One day, I left practice early because some of the girls were being extra mean to me. One of the girls, Alex, had been in my circle of friends since middle school. I thought she was still my friend. That afternoon, I sent her an AIM CHAT message telling her that I'd gone home to smoke a bong after practice.

But I shouldn't have trusted her. Alex had it in for me, and she framed me. She saved the conversation, printed it, and handed the printout to my coach and athletic director.

The next day when I went to practice, I was called into a meeting with my coach, my athletic director, and my mother. They told me that I wasn't allowed on the team anymore. I put two and two together and figured that Alex got me kicked off the team before competition season even started, and that was what

I loved about cheering—the competitions, not the games.

Not giving up, I invented a fake conversation that looked exactly like the one Alex had printed. In this made-up message, the coach was trying to sell me heroin. I printed this and handed it to the athletic director, saying, "Look how easy it is to make up fake stories and get someone in trouble. Obviously Coach doesn't sell heroin, so why would you just assume that this conversation was a truthful one and not a spiteful joke?"

That still didn't help. I was permanently kicked off the team when I still had two more years to go, and for malicious reasons. I continued fighting to stay on that squad, and no one helped. But I lost. I never wanted to leave.)

Back to the letter:

You wouldn't waste a Sunday horseback riding.

(Because you refused to keep driving me there on weekends when we moved so far away.)

It seems you run from thing to thing, and always drugs are involved.

(I don't even know what to say to that comment because it's so off-base. At seventeen years old, am I not supposed to be active and running around trying new things before I become an adult?)

These problems have been going on for a while now (the past 6 months).

We are worried about your future.

(Please, I have a 3.5 GPA and I am trying to go to UCLA, what the fuck are you worrying about my future for?)

We would love to see you thrive in whatever you want to do, but it is time for you to take some responsibility for your actions and decisions. We hope that this program will give you a chance without any distractions to take a look at Marissa and come to terms with her.

(I am perfectly fine with me. The problem is, YOU'RE not fine with me.)

We want you to accept authority, even when you don't agree, and not become confrontational. We want you to be able to put forth effort even when there is no immediate reward. Also, very important to both of us, is that you remain drug-free.

(I will sit here and tell these people what they want to hear so that I can go home and move on with my life. But it is an unrealistic request to think that I'm never gonna smoke a joint again, or take a puff of weed. It's just not gonna happen that way.)

We would like you to be happy and enjoy life, not just for the "fun" things,

(Isn't life about fun and happiness?)

but to appreciate everything around you, see the mountains, smell the flowers, take time out to appreciate things outside yourself.

(This whole year I've been growing and changing as a person. I am nowhere near the girl who stepped through the high school doors for the first time as a freshman. I have come so far as a person, and it's such a shame that my parents do not feel the same way or see any progress. Just focusing on the downfalls, you'll never see all the good. Bad is easy to judge; no one remembers the good, because it's not as noteworthy.)

We want you to be the best person you can be

(The best person YOU want me to be? Or the best person I want to be for me?)

and enjoy and thrive with the tremendous creative talents you have been blessed with.

Most of all, we would like you to treat us with love and support, as we have treated you.

(This is not support. This is a program designed to force me to conform to exact, arbitrary guidelines, to manipulate me to be so afraid of this ever happening again that I change to fit their mold.)

We love you very much and we know that you are exceptionally smart and strong and have the ability to overcome all these problems and develop into a wonderful human being.

(The problems you feel I have, I do not agree with. And life is not about my being the person you want me to be. It's about my being the person I want to be. Because every morning, I wake up with myself, not you.)

Please take this opportunity as a gift and work hard for yourself to make this a great experience in your life.

We love you very much,
Mom and Dad

———

Don't get me wrong. I understand that my parents love me and want only the best for me. But a barrier was drawn when they stopped accepting me and started trying to turn me into their own version of me.

My first day here, in the car heading to the doctor's office for my checkup, Anthony had warned me, "Beware of the impact letters." Now that's starting to make sense. My parents were clueless to me as a person anyway, but this letter sounds too calculated, as if someone detached from our family has revised it.

A week or so before I was taken, I wrote a commentary about our troubled family dynamics. I knew something had to give, but not this, not this way.

In this synthetic impact letter, my parents just sound dead and disengaged. These woods, this place where I've been dumped, are something I'm going to have to deal with by myself. There's absolutely no backup, no one reassuring me it's all going to be OK. Because everyone knows it isn't. Not these counselors. And not my parents either.

Day 9

Today is the first day I'll get to talk with Cara, my therapist. I've had a therapist before, and I know this interaction will have to be played right. In this first encounter, I'd like to get more information from her than she gets from me. I've been anticipating this meeting because she's going to be my only source of outside information. It's been nine days already, and I have so many questions about what's going on at home. And when I'm projected to go home. So many goddamn questions that I know are not going to be answered directly.

Cara is younger-looking than I expected, maybe around 28; tall and skinny, with brown hair and a soft face. She's not intimidating; in fact, she looks like this isn't the right job for her. It shows in her appearance, not in her face. She seems to be playing dress-up in pastel-colored hiking gear. As our eyes meet, she walks toward my spot on the ground.

I haven't yet figured out whose interests these people have in mind—mine, my parents', or theirs. Perhaps all three. Maybe my parents will come to their senses after reading my letter about how upset I am, and they'll come here and rescue me. Or maybe not. Truth is, it's a long shot that my parents will come to get me.

A few more strides, and Cara is by my side. She smiles

and sits Indian-style directly in front of me. Their smiles never seem sincere, although hers is slightly warmer and more sympathetic.

"Hi, Marissa. I'm Cara. How have you been adjusting so far?"

In my head: *Adjusting? You think I'm supposed to adjust to a place like this? Send me the fuck home, you crazy bitch.*

But to her, "Oh well, it's been really rough and I've been really homesick. I wanna go home but I'm trying as hard as possible to get all my stuff done so I can leave in 28 days."

"That sounds good," she says. "Don't try to rush through your hard skills because you still have to focus on yourself, you know."

"Yeah, I know. I am starting to look deeper into myself," I assure her. *Play the game.*

"Do you know why you're here?"

"I know why my parents sent me here." Out of the corner of my eye I see Lindsay watching us.

"Why do you think they sent you here?"

"Because they think I'm doing drugs and that I'm a belligerent, uncontrollable child who they don't feel is fit to have at home."

"Do you agree with them?" She's like one of those telemarketers who have lists of phrases for responding to whatever their victims say. It's all canned.

In my head: *Lady, do you think I agree with them?*

"No, I don't agree with them. But I know that they sent me here because they don't understand me, and they perceive me the wrong way."

She looks into my eyes. "Do you feel that what you were doing was wrong?"

I've got to make her understand what was really going on. "I smoked a little pot," I tell her. "I tried cocaine a few times, and I just for the first time had gained friends. For the first time in my life this past year I've experimented, or even got to hang out with the 'cool' kids, and now you're going to criticize me and chastise me for doing so?"

"I am not judging you for anything, Marissa." Another formulaic answer.

In my head: *I cannot get aggravated over what I feel is right. Because she's going to see that as a defense.*

"I'm just saying that I wasn't as bad as my parents thought I was," I say in a nice tone of voice. "My mother just worked in the high school and knew every single kid, so it didn't really give me a fair shot at friends, with my mother picking and choosing the 'good' ones."

"OK, OK. But didn't your parents mention something about an arrest?"

Now I have to admit it to her. She knows anyway. "I got arrested for possession of marijuana. It was less than 24 grams, and it was pot that wasn't even mine. I just happened to be there in the car with him when they nabbed this kid, and he wouldn't admit it was his. So we all got screwed. The cops kept telling me they were going to impound my car, and I did not know what impound meant and kept asking, 'Why would you crush my car?' thinking they meant 'compound'. Their scare tactics worked, and I blurted out 'It's not mine but it's in the glove compartment, please don't squish my car,' I pleaded with the state trooper detective in a plainclothes uniform."

In my head: *This doesn't sound good. But what am I going to say? I can't lie. I did get arrested. It also was not my stuff; objective fact.*

She sits a little straighter and looks more official. "All right. Well, now that I know a little more about you, we can start working on some things while you're here. The impact letter that you received from your parents was a way for them to get out all their feelings about what's been going on lately. As a homework assignment from me, I want you to write your accountability letter back to them by our meeting next week. In your accountability letter you must go over all points of interest mentioned in their letter to you. You need to take accountability for them, and mostly you really have to understand why and what you are taking accountability for, and what accountability is. Admit to yourself what is wrong, and admit it to them."

What a load of trivial work. "OK, I can do that."

"Also, I want you to work on this psych evaluation your parents wanted me to give you. They feel it will provide them help with understanding you better." She hands me the evaluation forms in an envelope.

"OK, that's fine," I agree. "I'd like to know as well what the psych evaluation would say." I rummage in my pack. "I almost forgot. Here's my letter to my parents, and a few to my friends. Please make sure to tell my parents to give my letters to my friends too. It's really important to me. And there's one in here for Molly, to try to motivate her to come back to the group."

In my head: *Even though it's more pleasant with Molly gone.*

"OK, I will get these letters out," she promises. "Thank you for the one to Molly. I'm sure she really appreciates your encouragement. Have a good rest of the day."

She rises gracefully, like a deer, and whisks away, seeming so at peace with her mission here. Which makes no sense in a place where peace and happiness are impossible.

"Hey," Lindsay calls over as soon as Cara is out of sight. "Did you get a psych evaluation?"

"Yeah, so?"

"You're *so* not going home after here," she informs me.

"What do you mean?" I answer. "Yes, I am. I'm going to be a senior, and I need to go to college."

Lindsay shakes her head. "Everyone who gets handed a

psych eval *never* goes home. It's like a 'must have' for boarding schools to see before they let you in so they know you're not completely insane. Or if you are, how to deal with you."

That can't be true. "I'm *not* going anywhere! I'm going home. I turn 18 not far into the year. My parents would not do that to me. I'm fine. All I did was smoke pot and be obnoxious. I think they can get over it."

"That's what *you* think," she says, rolling her eyes and looking away.

What a bitch.

Day 10

Between the rest of PT yesterday and last night and this morning, I finished my psych eval. Which is good, because I was not allowed to do any other work until I was finished with it. Which really took away time from working on my traps, which I'm almost finished with. I hope I can get all my traps done by tomorrow or on expo so I can request my TFG (transfer for growth) from Bear to Wolf.

I can't believe Lindsay was such a dream-crusher last night. I can't be going to boarding school. That psych eval is just for my parents' peace of mind that nothing is wrong with me.

Caroline snatches my pack from behind me. Jolted out of my thoughts, I thump to the ground and look up at her, annoyed. "Hey!"

She laughs and says, "Get up, we gotta go to the main cabin for the switch. It's instructor changeover."

"What's that?"

"All our counselors change once a week. They never stay the same for more than seven days."

"Well, that sucks," I tell her. "Doesn't it? I mean, I guess I would rather get to know them for longer, ya know?"

"Yeah, me too. There have been ones I've really liked. But

sometimes they rotate back every few weeks, maybe. If we're lucky." She shrugs with a halfhearted grin. "It sucks, just like no FI (future information), or no good food, or no beds, sucks. But it gets easier. Now get up, we gotta go."

Day 11

It's Day 11 now and we're supposed to go on another expo. These expos are awful. I'm not so good at hiking. My bug bites are throbbing, red and swollen this morning. Shoulda taken Benadryl last night to avoid this now.

Everyone's spread out eating lunch now. We're sitting in an area that Sarah (new instructor) calls Dunbar. It's swampy and hard to find dry ground here. I shove my pack underneath me to sit on so at least the clothes I'm wearing don't get soaked through. The trees are tall, dense, and dark, letting in only a few rays of sunlight. The air is muggy and smells musty. Circles of gnats swarm above like mini storm clouds.

Lindsay and Christine are off in a corner, gossiping about how shitty Dunbar is, which doesn't help me because now I'm just dreading it. I stepped in a lake earlier when we first started hiking through the swamp forest, and now my socks and boots are soaked. Which is the worst out here because it's not like we have a dryer on hand. We have a fire pit instead.

The new girl, Raquel, lacks some common sense. It's hard to bite my tongue when I'm talking to a person whose logic is that 2+2=5. She can't remember basic things and can't even answer the simplest questions. Raquel is 15 years old, black, and comes from Maryland. She's overly ADHD and can't for the life of her figure out why she's here. She's long and lanky and has an awkward gait.

Remember Gumbo, that tall, green, gangly sort-of cartoon-like character we all used to watch when we were kids? Well, that's who Raquel reminds me of, Gumbo minus a brain, if he ever had one to begin with. It's been hard for me to talk to her without looking astonished, giving away how stupid I truly think she is. I watch her with one eyebrow raised and my lip pulled back, looking confused and bewildered at the nonsensical sentences coming from her mouth, thinking to myself, *What are you saying?*

But then I stop and think, *Marissa, you are going to meet a sea of people exactly like this girl, so now you need to learn how to deal with them.* Right now, I was supposed to be at the UCLA summer program with really cool, talented theater kids, instead of out here in the woods with all these misfits, but that's not how the trajectory turned out now, is it?

A loud cackling noise from our new instructor, Sarah, distracts me from Raquel. Sarah and a few girls are sitting in a circle, laughing excitedly about something. Even Lindsay and Caroline have stopped gossiping, attracted by the laughter. Now we're all in the circle together, listening to Sarah tell funny stories about her dog. This is the first time I've sat around having a normal conversation, talking and laughing about something not related to being here, not about how bad we all are. Something so simple, a dog. But stories of that dog pull us out of the here and now, giving us a chance to relax for five minutes, and reminding us of real life. The life we're not living anymore.

Day 12

Smack! Right on my face, right into the ground. It's always hard to get up after you fall. Imagine falling face-first onto the dirt, followed by a 50-pound pack slapping into your back, pushing you down even harder, pressing you into the ground. Lindsay is right behind me in line, and she saw me fall. I suddenly feel her pulling on my pack, allowing me to get to my feet and keep going.

I've only just mastered getting my pack on alone. You turn the pack, shoulder straps facing you. Plant your right foot in front of your left for grounding. Bend down and grab each shoulder strap with a hand, and thrust the pack onto your knee for balance. Then quickly slide your right arm and shoulder into the strap while swinging to your right as hard as you can to get the pack to swing to your left side. The moment the pack gets to your left side, slide your left arm in quickly. Secure your balance, maybe leaning forward slightly, and then it's on!

The area we're hiking in is dense, with greens and mountains all around. Our trail is between two mountains and a ravine. To the right, the hill goes straight up at an almost 90-degree angle. To the left, the hill makes a steep slope down, steep enough that you do NOT want to slip down it.

Just now, when I slipped, I could have fallen off the trail. I shoot right up and keep going without a word. No one but Lindsay needs to know that I'm struggling.

Sweet Sarah from yesterday's lunch morphs into a military lesbian leader, barking orders all morning. Sporadically, she warns us while we're hiking, "If you complain, we just add more miles to the hike, so keep it up, girls. I love to hike."

Well, guess what, Sarah, I don't like to fucking hike! And then my mind checks itself and says, well, it's not really about what you want today, Marissa, is it. So I shut my mouth, hold it in, and keep on hiking for my sake and for the rest of the group's sake.

About a mile or so later, Sarah finally sits us down for lunch, the first break we've had in hours. Huffs and puffs and beaten-down expressions come from all the girls in the group. I feel bad for them. Even Lindsay, who's never shown any signs of weakness since I've been here, seems to be on her last strings.

A short fifteen minutes for lunch, and then Sarah's barking at us to get our packs on and check our group materials so we can get going.

Caroline taps me on the shoulder. "Marissa, were you carrying the billy cans for the group?"

"Yeah, why?"

"I think one's missing," she says, alarmed. "I see only three on your pack, and we need four."

"Fuck, this is gonna be like last time when Molly forgot the rope at the campsite before we took off."

"Yeah, probably," Caroline says. "But we better tell Sarah now so we don't go any farther without it."

"OK, I'll go," I say.

"Sarah, I think a billy can might have dropped off my pack while we were hiking," I say. "It could be only a quarter mile back, I think."

"Great, I'll send another instructor to follow you while you go retrace your steps. You just earned the group more lunchtime," she replies with a calm happiness. She, too, gets to relax for another ten minutes at least, while I retrace my steps.

This isn't exactly like what happened when Molly left the rope behind. I'm the only one who has to go back and search for the billy can. The rest of the group gets to sit and rest while I do it.

Fucking wonderful.

Day 13

Sarah is sitting up straight, looking excited. "Before we start hiking today, we are going to do something a bit differently," she announces. We're all staring in anticipation. No one knows what's going to be asked of us. She appears exuberant, but this can't be good news. I don't trust her. She gives weird vibes.

"Pack drills!" she bursts out.

Many sighs.

"What's a pack drill?" I ask.

"Instead of regular morning call," Sarah begins, "We're going to start with just our personal tents and belongings. I am going to time it, and you all need to have everything packed and ready to hike within three minutes." She looks happy. *Sadistic bitch.*

That's not possible, I think. Everyone's faces drop. Last night after our hike, we found a campground that was less than ideal. It was hilly, not flat; the ground was moist; and bushes and shrubs were covering everything. There was no near water source that we could find, and it got so dark that we needed to camp.

Packing up this camp isn't going to be easy, let alone in a three-minute personal pack drill.

"If you don't all get it done in three minutes the first time," Sarah continues, "We will keep unpacking and repacking as many times as it takes to get it right. OK?" She smiles wide as if this is some sort of fun game. To her, maybe it is, but didn't she already put us through enough shit yesterday during our hike, barking orders and commands? Didn't she get her power trip then? What's the purpose of this? How is it supposed to improve us, all these cruel orders imposed on us with no warning?

We all scatter to our tents to look over our knots and figure out the best way to shove all our shit into our packs in a hikeable condition.

My tent is tied A-frame between two trees. The ground underneath is on an incline, and everything is damp from morning dew and grass. My knots are tight; I made sure of that last night because I was afraid of getting rained on. It's going to take some work to undo these knots. I take a look at my pack, which was small to begin with. I've gotten pretty competent at traveling as light as possible. It usually takes me a decent amount of time to organize my stuff in there properly so I can hike comfortably, considering that I'm new to hiking.

This is one of those assignments where you're practically guaranteed to fail. Waves of anxiety start in my chest and run through my body. My breathing is getting heavy and pushing down on my chest. My tear ducts are swelling up, ready to burst any minute. I'm frozen, staring at my pack, knowing I'm not going to be able to do this in three minutes. And why, in real life, would anyone have to do this in three minutes? But this is not real life.

I just can't take this abuse anymore, I think. What kind of parents would want to put their child through this? It's terrible when this happens during wars, when families and kids have to hike long distances over rough terrain, trying to find a safe place. This is like an artificial war in which these so-called instructors impose one hopelessly frustrating punishment after another on their helpless victims. If we were dogs, the ASPCA would have been called in long ago.

I drop my head back and look up into the sky, holding back the tears and the misery, because I know I'll be holding up the group for not being able to do this on my first shot, or even the second. I don't know how long it'll take me to learn to pack my shit in three minutes. Once the first tear falls, I know that all the emotions will run through me.

"Ready, set, go!" Sarah yells.

My hands immediately go to work on the knots holding up my blue tarp. Pulling, pulling, pulling away, they all seem stuck. Folding the blue tarp, ground mat, and bug nets eats up a lot of time and ends up messy anyway. I try shoving it all into my pack. It won't fit. I rip it all out and try shoving it in again. Still won't fit.

"Time's up!" Sarah shouts.

"Fuck!" I let out a frustrated scream.

"Did I hear you say a curse word, Marissa? Yelled over a co-instructor?"

I roll my eyes and see another instructor walking toward me.

"That's gonna be five alternative words now," she orders.

They have this rule here where if you swear, you need to say five alternative words you could have used instead of the curse word.

I feel like cursing more and louder. Instead, I say, "Fudge, firefly, stone, bug, annoyed! Good?" My blood is starting to boil and my tears are still welled up behind their dam.

"That'll do," she says, and strides away.

"Again!" Sarah screams, louder than before. "Because some of you have not finished on time, you all have to set up your tents again and we need to redo this drill."

Now we are doing drill? I want to cry out the word *fuck* fifty more times, as loud as possible. This is moronic busy work. We're accomplishing nothing.

We all redo our tents, obediently, like robots. This time I make sure that my knots are much looser so I halfway have things ready to go.

"And AGAIN!" she signals us to start the drill.

I start ripping away at the strings and mats and personal items like my journal and my extra clothes and crocks. Shoving this stuff into my pack, I keep in mind that this pack has to be hikeable. This time, it's easier to get the tarp down, but I have to fold it, otherwise it won't fit.

"Time's up!"

I look down. Everything is half hanging out, and half the stuff is not even touched. My pent-up tears finally burst loose and start streaming down my face, and all the muscles in my body instantly tense up. I drop what was in my hands and squeeze my fists tight. My breathing is getting heavy and I feel myself beginning to break down. I try to take a deep breath but it feels as if there's a stone pressing down on my chest, making it hard to inhale.

"I can't do this," I cry out. "I can't. I'm done. Go on without me. Like you did to Molly. God knows where she is right now." Tears are flooding my face.

"Come on, Marissa, you can do this," offers Lindsay.

"No," I snap back with fire in my eyes. "I don't want to." Anger is surging through me now. So angry with this stupid fucking drill, and so angry that I'm even standing here in these woods, way out in bumblefuck.

What if I just stop? Completely refuse to move? I want to.

All the girls are yelling over to me, "Let's go, Marissa." One of them says, "You've been doing so well, what's wrong right now?" Another says, "Let's just get this done so we can keep moving."

My feet are planted on the ground and I'm staring at all my unpacked shit all over the place, with tears blurring my vision. I'm not moving. My body won't let me. It's as if my mind has decided that I can't allow myself to hurt me anymore. This is all just too much. Why? Why me? Why and how could my parents do this? Do they know what we have to go through out here? My angry thoughts are screaming in my head; wanting to ask these questions, but knowing they are unanswerable.

I just can't.

Day 14

Yesterday, 20 minutes after I stopped moving, I slapped myself in the face and came to the cold realization that my situation was still not going to change, and it still didn't matter how much I willed it not to be true. I am not Molly, and I needed to move.

When I redid my tent, I made sure that all the knots were undone and all my stuff was folded so I didn't have to waste any time. I threw everything into the pack within two minutes that time. All the anger pushed me to shut up and do it, and fast. I threw my pack over my shoulder and kept hiking.

We hiked to a shockingly nice campsite today. The ground is completely flat. The trees are perfectly spread out for our tents. And there are pine needles everywhere, falling from above, creating a floor of sorts to sit on. Close by, behind our group tarp, is water—a beautiful lake that we could wade into, if we're allowed.

On the horizon is another campsite, with store-bought tents, a fire pit going, and kids running in and out of the water, carelessly. Wouldn't it be nice to be them right now.

I'm done giving fake smiles to these people. Maybe it seems like I'm not getting anywhere because I'm not really showing how I feel. I don't know how to play this game anymore. Perhaps I never did. These people, I don't understand what they want from us. All these tasks, games, and drills are fragmented. Their logic doesn't seem to follow any pattern that I've noticed.

I still need to do my traps. I'm falling behind. This was not my original plan.

Day 15

It's the Fourth of July.

We left expo today, only to get shuttled out on another one. I can feel property getting closer. While we're hiking, we're staying inside lines marked off by symbols on certain trees, the same faded red plastic flags as on property.

The grass is denser now. No slick pine needles, and flat ground. We're trudging through damp, tall grass under the beating sunshine. I imagine what we must look like, walking in one long straight line with our bright-red long pants and orange fleeces, walking sticks in hand.

A bit suspect, I must presume. Or primitive. Looking like well-behaved prisoners going on a nice hike through the mountains, we trudge on, but we're only just us troubled children sent to be fixed.

We duck out of the sunlight and thick grass and into a forest of tall trees and downed branches, leading into trees so high that you can't see some of their tops. They're blocking any sunlight that would allow grass to grow thick. Our head instructor, Sarah, is sizing up the space around her, probably searching for the right spot for setting up the group tarp. We need a big open space, but through this tangle of jungle trees and vines, there's little open space. Sarah points west and follows her sight line to a decently sized clearing, where she throws her pack on the ground and drops down on top of it.

"Today is the Fourth of July," she informs us.

As if we don't know. We all mark down the days in our journals, or at least I do. It's the only way to keep track of how many days we've each been here and what the actual date is. All the girls either roll their eyes or sigh. We're aware that today is the Fourth of July. Most of us had traditions on this date, or engagements we were looking forward to, that we're missing because we're stuck in this program. We don't want to be reminded by Sarah, of all people, that today is a holiday that's meaningless to us out here.

My family doesn't have traditions. They don't really have any interest in holidays. We never do much on holidays except for Hanukkah, when I get presents. But we never have formal family get-togethers; not even family dinners. We go out to dinner on occasion, but I've never experienced my mother in the kitchen calling upstairs, "Dinner's ready." In spite of that, I like holidays. I've always believed that they give people a reason to come together and celebrate. Celebrate anything.

"I love the Fourth of July!" Raquel shouts, half dancing in place and smiling from ear to ear.

Raquel, as a person, just aggravates me.

"I'm sure you're all not very happy about being here right now," Sarah begins. But then she drops it, just like that. Not another mention; no discussion about how we're feeling about it. The only good thing about right now is that we've arrived at our campsite early, leaving us some extra PT. That might be promising.

"For this night call, we're not going on a water run because it's too far," Sarah says. "So we'll go after call, as a group, down to find water. You all have 30 minutes. Go."

Call seems easy so far, except for finding a spot to sleep. The trees are too close together, making it difficult to find a spot where my personal tarp will fit between two of them. We all work as a group and plop back down in the center of the group tarp, right on time.

"Change of plans," Sarah announces. "Grab your day packs. We're going on a short hike."

That's one of the most infuriating aspects of this whole miserable experience—that someone can just suddenly decide what you're going to do, when and how you're going to do it. And "it" is usually something unpleasant and strenuous. There are no "short hikes" around here.

"Seriously!" I protest. "I thought we were getting water, eating lunch, having PT, and getting a break for once."

"Well, now you're not. So let's go." She smiles at me.

Sarah ends up hiking us two miles to property to eat lunch and shower. We really need showers; all of us are filthy. We don't get a change of clothes every day. Each of us has two of everything, and we wear these clothes for a whole week straight. When we get back to property, we wash all our clothes during shower time in the industrial laundry machines at the infirm.

This is the first time I've seen the showers, and I'm grossed out by the shower walls. They scare me beyond belief. Not only are they filthy and disgusting, but they're so close to you that there's no room to move inside the shower without touching all the walls. I have a pet peeve or phobia about showers in general. They have to look brand-new or at least extremely clean, and have enough room for me to wash without touching the walls or smacking into them. Even the small curtains are covered in what looks like ancient slime. I hate curtains too, because the sometimes they touch you in the shower. If I had it my way, it would be either an open shower or an unmovable door.

Another instructor barks out the rules of the showers. "You have only three minutes each. We will go in three sets of two. You must deep-clean the bathrooms, including the showers, toilets, floors, walls, and sinks, before we leave. All must be approved before leaving. If this is not done properly, you will lose your shower privileges."

Uh oh. The most futile anxiety attack of my life has begun. "I'm not going in the showers," I blurt out. "They are disgusting and gross and I feel less clean going in than if I just stay here for the three minutes you're allowing me in water. I just can't. It's making me freak out. I can't."

"Marissa, you have to," Sarah insists.

"I don't care anymore what I have to do. You can't make me, and I'm not going in."

She crosses her arms and glares at me. "This will just reflect badly on you if you do not do this and cooperate."

So be it, I don't care. My heart starts pounding and I feel paralyzed. I will explain to Cara why I just can't go in there. I refuse to force myself to have more anxiety over this for three minutes in a revolting and slimy shower cave.

Sarah shrugs, rolls her eyes, and walks away.

The others in the group take showers as ordered. And I refuse to join in their cleanup activity because I didn't take part in this whole gross bathroom experience.

When I say that these bathrooms are less than sanitary, I'm not telling the whole story. They are worse than the men's room in Port Authority at four in the morning. There's rust in the corners and around the drains. The stench of vomit and urine is everywhere, masked by the scent of bleach.

Everyone is supposed to clean the bathroom before hiking again, yet I'm watching my group half-ass clean everything. How clean can it ever be if everyone who uses it half-ass cleans up after themselves? There's no way I'm going to step inside, let alone go into that shower naked and barefoot.

And that's not all that's disgusting about living in the woods. We're teenage girls, and we have periods. They give us pads, but we have to ask for them when we need them. Because the camping rule is "Don't leave a trace," we can't just bury used pads in the woods. We have to wrap them in toilet paper and stuff them in our packs to carry back to the infirm with us, whenever we get back there. Which means sometimes carrying dirty pads around for days.

I consider again, much as I did the other day with the pack drills, what it would be like to stop moving as Molly did. At least I'm on property now, not out in the woods, so it's a safer environment to stop. They wouldn't have to hike me anywhere. I'm already at the intake office. It would be impossible, I imagine, for them to physically force me to walk. What would they do? Lift me up arm by arm, throw my pack on my back, and push from behind? They could leave me alone to scare me, but they can't make me move.

I sit glued to the bench. I'm gonna do it again. I'm going to tell them "No more," and I'll really stop this time. If I'm going to stop anywhere, here is where it needs to be. On property, right in front of the infirm building. With showers, shelter, food, phone lines, and people other than my group. If I stop moving right here, right now, it will cause a huge scene and mess up everyone's schedule. Other groups won't be able to pull up to the infirm because they aren't allowed to see other campers. The people who work in the office won't know how to handle the situation. And they'll be forced to call my parents and tell them I'm sitting right here next to them. My parents for sure will want to talk to me.

They're all ignoring me. I sit here glued to the bench, in tears, not speaking to anyone, debating with myself what to do. Tears silently stream down my face, as they did the night I sat helplessly in my bed with the escorts.

The other girls finish their showers and their cleanup, and they all start to head back to the campsite. I don't know what's going to help me. It appears that nothing really will.

So badly do I *not* want to continue. Wishing I could just get a phone call; anything.

Thirty minutes later my bodily functions take over and I become hungry; starving. Still in tears, I force myself to get up and walk the two miles back to camp, alone.

Sarah is barking out orders again. "Before we hike back to property, we gotta do this water run together because it's so far away, OK, girls?"

We all moan. It's going to be a lot of work.

This campsite is rather interesting, with tall trees everywhere and little hills all around. It's hard to catch your bearings. Last night at the bear hang, we got lost getting back to camp. All the trees look the same, and for some reason we camped far from our water source and bear hang. It was impossible to get back alone. We were constantly looking at the compass; it was almost comical.

Sometimes it's frightening in the dark. You feel like something's going to pop out and grab you. I was always afraid of the dark, and no one else is here but us. Now that I've learned firsthand how hard it is to live in the woods, I doubt that any murderers or child molesters are lurking in the backwoods just waiting for the lonely camper to breeze by.

Once again in our straight line of girls, we saunter down to the lake together. None of us likes being in charge of water runs because it wastes time and you have to be precise. You're not allowed to just drop your Nalgene into the water and let it fill up, because you'd be at risk for all the diseases floating in the water. So the instructors make us carry around a water pump. It's small, with a black tube that goes into the water, attached to what looks like an old perfume dispenser.

This is the procedure: you sit with the tube in the water and the pump over the opening of a Nalgene. You pump water into each individual Nalgene, one at a time, and then drop in two tablets of iodine to further sanitize the water. There are two water bottles for each girl, plus two for each instructor, or 20 Nalgenes altogether. The whole process takes around 45 minutes. Forty-five minutes of the girls sitting together and complaining, or talking about what's possibly going to happen later today, or what we're going to have for lunch. Stupid "kill time" talk. But this nonsensical talking among seven immature "troubled teens" never leads to anything productive. Somebody always offends somebody else, or says the wrong thing, or gets in trouble over an unguarded revelation. Forty-five minutes of unstructured free time is a guaranteed recipe for trouble.

During the shower debacle yesterday, I saw Raquel laughing with another new girl, Kassandra, who arrived yesterday. Curious about what was so funny, I took a couple of steps closer to them so I could see what they were messing around with. They were holding water bottles that had just been filled and they were drinking from them, conspicuously spilling out some of the water.

The thing I forgot to mention about the water is that no one likes drinking it all. ALE has rules that nearly drown us in water. They feel that it's unsafe for us to drink a minimal amount of water because of the heat and strenuous hiking. So they require us to drink four full 32-ounce Nalgenes per day. Each bottle holds the equivalent of four large coffee mugs full of water. All four Nalgenes combined add up to a gallon of water a day. Picture 16 large coffee mugs of water in one day, and you understand the difficulty. I wonder if our bodies were meant to process all this water.

Your first water bottle has to be finished by the end of morning call, which is only 20 to 40 minutes maximum after you wake up. Then you have to drink two more during the day and one for night call. That doesn't seem like a lot, but these bottles are huge and no one can ever drink the mandatory amount. We all pour our water on the ground whenever we can sneak the opportunity—while brushing our teeth, or packing, or hiking, so no one can see. No one wants to miss a call because of a ridiculous water-bottle requirement.

On this particular occasion, we are done with morning call and we're just filling up bottles before the hike.

I stand silent for another few minutes observing Raquel and Kassandra. They're spilling water again. The thing is, I like Kassandra, and I really don't want Raquel screwing up her progress with her retarded ways of getting around the rules. If Raquel were teaching Kass how to drip water out of the bottle inconspicuously, that would be fine. But she isn't, and she's putting the whole group at risk.

"Raquel, what are you doing?" I ask.

"Hee hee, nothing," she says, turning her back to me.

"Raquel, I'm standing right here. I'm not blind. What are you doing?"

She makes a face at me. "I'm not doing anything. Leave me alone."

Her stupidity infuriates me. "Raquel, you've been here for only a few nights, and you're already trying to get around the rules when you're only a few feet away from the instructors. What is wrong with you?"

All I want is to go home. Watching this girl jeopardize my goal makes me mad. Ever since she's been here, she has contributed nothing; if anything, she's held us back because she's new and not used to the long hikes. She still doesn't know why she's here, and neither do the rest of us.

Raquel's impact letter last night was a joke. It was her high-class black family from Maryland telling her that she needs to grow up, and learn, and become an adult. They feel that this Leadership Expedition camp will teach her the skills to do so. Except that her parents don't realize that they're sending her into the woods with a group of so-called "troubled adolescents." We aren't here for learning curriculum for school.

Raquel doesn't need ALE. What she really needs is a tutor, and to be dropped a grade in school so she can catch up. Her social skills and learning abilities are way below what they should be, and she probably has some sort of learning disability. She's the only girl in the group who's using the program's lesson books for school credit, which she needs because she failed so many classes as a high school freshman. Science was hard for Raquel in high school, and her parents figure that being out in the woods will help strengthen not only her social and leadership skills, but her outdoor science skills as well. I suppose whoever her parents spoke to on the phone about the program sold it as a great learning experience. But learning to live off the land and leave no trace is far from an in-depth environmental science study.

I don't know what her parents were thinking. I guess they told her that she isn't going to be here for very long, and she mentions that at every convenient moment. Her parents dropped her off, and all that Raquel would say about the program was, "Well, I know I'm going home soon, so it doesn't matter anyway. All I have to do is finish my science lessons."

The fact that this girl thinks she's here for a science lesson, while I'm not sure when I'm ever going to see a real bed again, doesn't sit right. If Raquel is going to do anything productive here, it better be respecting the group that she doesn't feel she belongs in to begin with. At least for our sanity. Because the rest of us don't know what's going to happen next, or even if we're going to whatever "home" means anymore.

"Nothing's wrong with me!" she shoots back. "I'm just doing what I want."

Kassandra backs away, realizing that this isn't going to end well.

"Raquel, stopped spilling your water out right in front of everyone," I tell her. "It already takes us forty-five minutes to fill the Nalgenes. Don't make it longer and harder because we have to keep refilling your bottles three and four times. It's not fair," I plead with her.

"I'm not doing anything," she shouts back.

I felt like I'm talking to a person who has only a few automated, meaningless responses in her repertoire.

"Two plus two equals four, you idiot! Yesterday, during your program lesson on math, you kept getting it wrong because two plus two equals motherfucking four!" I yell at her. A couple of instructors come over when they hear us arguing.

"What's going on?" Mike asks.

I know I should think before I speak but… "Raquel is just so fucking stupid! I cannot bear it anymore." I shout this so loudly that everyone stops moving.

Dan says, "Five alternative words, Marissa."

"Fine! Idiot, moron, rock, wall, empty!"

"Idiot and moron don't count," Mike says.

"Fudge, freaking," I offer him. For my own satisfaction, I say them like curses. "Better?"

"Yes. Now, what's going on?" Mike asks Raquel and me.

"I'm not doing anything wrong." Raquel smiles like a dumbass, the smile of a person who you know is wrong, but who really thinks she is pulling the wool over your eyes.

Dan and I look at Raquel blankly. Mike is an asshole,

but he's not blind. He knows that she's always trying to get around the rules.

"Dan," I say, "She was pouring her water out right next to you, thinking she can get away with it. I understand she feels special, and thinks she's going home after her science lessons, but it's uncalled for and unfair for her to compromise the rest of the group because she doesn't want to do something."

"Raquel," Dan says. "Is this true?"

She puts on that goofy smile. "It's not as bad as it sounds."

1 2 N O O N

In the infirm building, on property, in the same small white room where they stripped me naked on my first day here, sits a stumpy woman at a table. In front of her is a set of cards with symbols on them. I walk in and sit on the other side of the table directly in front of her.

"I'm here to give you the second part of your psych evaluation," she says, without offering me her hand or even telling me her name.

Wonderful, I think.

I already took the first part of the psych eval at the campsite last week on a Scantron where you have to bubble in the correct letter. It consisted only of questions relating to thoughts and emotions, such as: Have you ever heard voices in your head telling you to harm yourself? Do you like yourself? Do you love your parents? Do you have thoughts of suicide? Do you have thoughts of homicide? Do you think you abuse drugs? Do you use drugs for self-medication? Do you consider drugs, including marijuana, to be harmful? Are you sad right now?

Today's portion of the evaluation is all cognitive thinking and learning questions. There are also some IQ tests I've never seen, and tests of memory, mathematics tests, and other fun stuff.

For four hours I sit facing this woman, parroting back numbers in the correct order, doing multiplication problems in my head, and taking other tests. I even do that typical movie test where they hold up ink blots and ask what you associate with each one.

4 : 1 3   P . M .

"We're done," the woman says. "You're allowed to use the bathroom located directly across from this room if you need to before we hike you back to your group."

"Thank you." I shake her hand and walk into the bathroom. I'm definitely going to take advantage of a toilet bowl I can sit on, rather than the hole in the ground I've become accustomed to squatting over.

I wonder how I did on all those tests.

I wonder if the results will make any difference.

Day 18

Instructor changeover day finally rids us of Sarah! There's a breath of fresh air with these new ones: Allison, Pete, and Mike.

We leave property today for another expo, hiking a long, winding trail that's so challenging it's taking forever to hike. The hikes get to be fun when they turn into obstacle courses. Even so, this trail is a lot easier than most because we aren't bushwhacking.

Near the end of the hike, we're stopped by a river, way bigger than the little creeks and streams we've come across on other hikes. A few big rocks jutting out from the rushing water form a pathway across. We slide down a hill and prepare to cross, descending cautiously on our packs.

"I think our packs are going to be too heavy to balance with over these wet rocks," I tell Pete. He seems like an OK guy.

"I was thinking the same thing," he says. "I just wasn't sure. Yeah, maybe you're right. Allison," he calls. "We need to cross without the packs first."

"Then make an assembly line to bring them over," she answers.

"OK. Girls, did you hear?" Pete says. "Let's drop the packs here, and whoever thinks she's the strongest goes first."

I'm already standing at the back of the line with Pete, so I stay behind with him to take care of the packs while everyone else crosses the rocks first. Most of the girls are safely on the other side, but Lindsay, Kassandra, and Caroline are standing on the rocks, waiting for Pete and me to hand them the packs, which they hand across. One by one, they step over the rocks and cross the river. Then I cross the rocks, followed by Pete.

We all catch our breath, grab our packs, and start hiking again. Near the path, just a few feet up the trail, there's a lean-to, which is a small hut for hikers to camp inside of instead of on the bare ground. Hallelujah, praise the mother-fucking Lord! There's a lean-to! For the first time in 18 days, I'll get to sleep on a floor with a roof overhead, instead of on the ground with a tarp one foot from my face.

"This is where we're camping, guys," Pete announces. "So get comfortable, and enjoy. You've got a lot of PT right now for your personal growth."

These words could not sound any sweeter right now! I need the time, desperately. I've already sparked all my fires, but I still cannot for the life of me get my trap line set up.

The fires weren't too bad. You're given a piece of charcoal cloth. Then you take a three-inch-long chunk of metal, about 1/3 inch thick, and smack it onto a rock to generate tiny sparks. You do this until one of the sparks hits the charcoal cloth and creates a small coal, or red spot, to turn into a flame. Next, you wrap the charcoal cloth with the red spot in something small and dry enough to catch fire quickly. Dry, crumbled leaves would work, or some dried pine needles from the ground under the trees. You wrap this all in a thin piece of birch wood bark and blow lightly into the cylinder, hoping to make the red spot grow and catch a flame. Without suffocating the coal, you blow this all into a fire.

Traps are much more challenging. They're not incredibly more difficult, but they're technical. My trap line is the last thing I need in order to request a transition to Wolf. Which will get me closer to going home. We're required to set three single traps, and I've already done that. But the trap line means three traps in a row that all go off perfectly. All three traps have to fall, not just one of them, to complete the line. Our traps are similar to real ones intended to catch animals, but ours are smaller versions. If we were making them full-size, they would theoretically work on any game we needed to trap and eat for survival.

On top of that, you have to make up word analogies to support your traps. You're supposed to relate components of the trap to your own behavior and the state of mind you were in back home, doing the things that you were sent here because of. It's time-consuming, and it's aggravating because I feel stupid writing them.

Here are some examples of these analogies:

Example 1: Smoking weed = bait stick: being relaxed and having fun. Running from problems.

The bait stick is what lures the animal into the trap. This is the program's parallel for why we chose to engage in activities that caused us to end up here. According to this reasoning, for me, the bait stick was smoking weed. The analogy exercise requires you to explain why the activity lured you, similar to how the bait stick of the actual trap lures the animal.

I hate doing traps anyway, so my example doesn't go any further than being relaxed and having fun. I'm throwing in "running from my problems" to make the instructors think I truly feel this way about my situation. But the truth is that I was never running from any problems when I smoked pot. If anything, pot brought together a lot of people who would never normally talk or interact with each other. It was a social catalyst in my life.

Example 2: Dead fall: bad relationship with parents, killing brain cells, slower short-term memory.

The dead fall is the part of the trap that falls when the animal goes for the bait. It keeps the animal in the trap and prevents it from running out.

Therefore, the dead fall is analogous to whatever bad consequences came from your bait. In my case, the bait was smoking weed. My parents didn't approve, which created a stressed relationship.

The next part of my analogy was there for the instructors—the killing of brain cells, and my slower short-term memory. But I know that those aren't caused by pot. My smoking pot is not going to make me any stupider than I was before. It's true that while you're high, short-term memory isn't as sharp as when you're sober. But weed doesn't affect long-term memory at all. You're just a bit clumsy for that time period. It also affects people differently. I'm not a man, so I don't have to worry about lowering my sperm count, which is a possible side effect.

For the second time, my parents have me psychologically evaluated in the wilderness, and my results come back totally normal except that my short-term memory is the slowest part of my learning. I'm sure that my parents blame this on smoking pot, which makes no sense at all. You definitely are not stoned while you take this test. So no one really knows why my short-term memory is the slowest part. I've been an actor my entire life and haven't ever had any problems remembering my lines.

Example 3: Post: not realizing it was hurting me. Having fun, being with friends, and not caring about consequences.

The post holds the entire trap together. The instructors want you to look at your life and analyze what made it easy for you to continue whatever activity you were doing; like the post holding the dead fall in the trap, before the entire thing came crumbling down and we all ended up in the woods.

My post analogy is that I just didn't care what people

thought about me or what I was doing. And I never thought that my parents would come to this. But I guess we are all wrong sometimes.

Example 4: Lever: not caring about parents' concerns. Having a "nothing can hurt me" attitude.

The lever of the trap is what snaps to break the dead fall and let it trap the animal. My parallel is that after my not caring for a while, someone else, my parents, finally fired back.

———

I have to do three of these long examples to finish Wolf phase. That means I have to write down three of them and then explain them to the instructors. After that, I have to make all three of my traps fall perfectly on one shot; otherwise, I'll have to redo them. All three have to work.

While I'm working away alone at my trap set, everyone else is making friendship bracelets. They're improvising them from extra twine we had for the traps. No one offers me one. Yesterday's public argument with Raquel must not have gone over well.

I write a letter to my best friend, Megan. I find out later that a lot went down with her when I was gone. She got depressed and didn't know how to handle herself. During our junior year, she and I had a breakthrough conversation where we discussed a lot of her problems and how to work on them; specifically, lying, which led to stealing. I've been really her only true friend who always has her back. So many people teased her. I find out later that when I left for ALE, she became addicted to cocaine.

I know that my mom told my friends what happened to me. They would not let my mom have me disappear without an explanation. I find out later that she told my friends I was sent to a place to get better. But my letters to them reveal how I'm really feeling, and my friends get a better understanding of where I am. I mail all my letters to my mom and she gives them out to my friends.

While I'm out here in the woods, the only mail I ever get is from my parents. No mail from anybody else, and no phone calls at all. Much later, my friends tell me that they would all wait for my letters and then read them together.

Dear Megan,

I feel like shit. My group hates me. The girls insist I use big words to make them feel stupid. That's just not true. I'm nearly 18 and some of them just hit 14. Plus, there's a difference in intelligence that isn't my fault. I have no choice but to "personally grow." The instructors say that's what has been holding me back from finishing Bear phase. That, along with the trap line that I can't figure out. I always run out of PT to finish.

I don't know what I'm supposed to be changing about myself when I disagree with my parents about the reasons why I am here. I miss home, and you, and my bed. Tell Goli I say Hi.

I hope he isn't in Israel yet. And tell all the girls I say Hey and I miss and love them.

Hopefully things can get better with Cara so she feels I'm ready to move forward. We've been getting nowhere in our sessions. Every time I get a letter from my parents, it's just an extension of my impact letter, no new news.

I feel like I'm reliving middle school. We hated middle school, remember? We were all such bitches and spoke Pig Latin to keep others out of certain conversations. We were fun.

Short letter. Needed to check in.

Love you sister, like a million stars,

Savage Gould

Day 19

Phew, finally.

I finished my trap line! Bear is always the longest phase, everyone says. No doubt Wolf will be shorter. I'm one step closer to graduation from this program and going home. At least today I can breathe a sigh of relief, and just wait to move forward. It's only nine more days until the 28-day minimum stay...

Day 20

The girls in the group hate me. We spent an entire truth circle discussing what I was doing wrong, or what I was doing that upset the girls and made it difficult for us all to get along. They just bashed me. It was like a middle school guidance counselor session where Mrs. Ellie Zerling would sit our "group of friends" down after pulling us out of class, and try to mediate why we were all arguing with each other. This happened when one of us would go down and complain about another, prompting this mediation session. Much like the girls in the group who complained about me.

Now we're hiking up a mountain. Gripping onto the mountain with my hands in the dirt and my feet securely on rocks, I duck my head away from the gravel and dirt sliding down toward me. Looking up, the only thing in sight is more mountain, up and up for as far as you can see, with no summit in view.

"Ow!" Christine calls from a bit up ahead.

"Are you okay?" Pete yells from right behind me.

"I fell and hit my knee," she says. "I'm bleeding, I need a Band-Aid."

Pete hurries up the trail ahead of me to help Allison with Christine. Everyone takes this window of opportunity to find an open spot on the rocks and plop down for a quick breather. We took daypacks and hiked from the lean-to straight up this mountain. The lean-to was conveniently located right at the entrance to the upward trail. It seems like we've been hiking forever up a mountain with no summit.

This extra-strenuous hike is certainly taking a toll on me. Ever since the first week of hiking, I've been pretty good at day-hiking up mini mountains. But this surely is no mini mountain. The sign at the trailhead down below says that we're on a back path up Whiteface Mountain. And this is definitely not a typical trail. There's no flat ground—it's just up, and up some more. Not flat up—rocky up. We're all becoming rock climbers this sunny afternoon. You can only tell it's sunny through small openings in the rocks and trees up ahead. The blue sky shining through the trees gives us momentum to reach the top.

We climb for an hour at a time, thinking that we're reaching the peak, only to have the path open up to another false peak, leading up to still more rocks to jump over. Right now we're sitting in one of those open false peaks. It was once a gigantic rock with several cracks in it, and it looks like it's been eroded over centuries. This is a desert of rocks in the middle of the lush mountain's white face.

"Take five, girls; we all need a break," Mike says.

For the first time on this hike, we all see the light from inside the tall trees. It's breathtaking, looking out and seeing hundreds of mountains for miles around. Some are snow-capped, others bright green; some are steep, and some lower. A couple of mountains we've hiked on the last expo are in the mountain range too, which Pete points out to us.

We're each allowed one disposable camera. I take mine out and start snapping pictures to preserve memories of this vast, boundless wilderness. Along with reverence for this overwhelming beauty is the feeling of deep hurt that I can't share this experience with the friends I love. I very much wish Mark could be with me.

"This was the first false summit, girls, let's get going," an instructor calls.

And up we go, past the desert of rock into another forest of tall trees. We pass a second false summit about an hour later. Then an hour after that, we hit the final summit, the real thing.

At the top of the mountain, there's a gift shop, right in the middle of the wilderness! And a long car trail leads down to the bottom. This whole time we've been climbing up the back of this peak, ragged and exhausted, our bus could have driven us to the top. But what fun would that have been?

People with binoculars are scattered around, looking out onto the same mountains that I admired earlier. Baseball caps, sunscreen, children laughing. It's nice to see those sights during this stressful time. I want to go talk to the people and have normal interactions, and maybe send out a distress call for help.

But Pete, Allison, and Mike are following protocol, keeping us a safe distance away from these happy, normal, free people and their families.

I'm inside a glass jar through which I can see the outside, but not leave. Trapped. The real world is only teasing me.

Day 21

Coming down from Whiteface takes half the time it did climbing up. It was a relief to stumble out of the thick trees directly into the lean-to last night. Two nights in a row in a lean-to as opposed to on the ground was glorious, but today we head out. No pack drills, just morning call.

In our regular hiking line, we trudge the same trail we took to get to the bottom of the mountain. Up and down hill lines with bushes and trees, with nothing in our way but dirt. No one complains or cries out to stop. After yesterday's excursion, we all seem to be coming together as hikers a bit better. The instructors know when we need a five-minute breather. Not stopping every two minutes makes our pace much quicker.

"Think we're camping out one more day or going back to property?" Kassandra asks me.

"I'm not sure," I tell her. "Maybe a campsite because of the lean-to for two nights?"

"I'm not sure. But hopefully we'll be there soon."

Suddenly we hear Caroline from the front of the line scream, "BUS!"

An exhale of relief. Property! And property a day early, even. Our bus takes us right to the showers, which I do in fact take this week. Whiteface was too much. I need to wash. It doesn't matter how disgusting the shower walls are. As for the cleanup chores, I'll just half-ass the cleaning like every-body else and not really do much. It's about time I learn to cut corners at this place. Raquel's not the only one who gets a free pass. Screw this!

I'm finally done with everything I need in order to move up to Wolf. I've been trying to offer smiles and encouraging words to the girls so Cara can believe I'm ready to move on.

It's Day 21, which is one week shy of 28. Maybe I still can finish this program in 28 days, finish up summer, and start my senior year on time with the rest of my class. It all seems promising. I don't care if it's 29 or 30 days, just as long as it's around 28.

I still haven't heard from my parents about my SAT scores, and I still don't know if my close friend Golan has joined the Israeli army already. I just need to stay positive so I can move forward and go home. Blinders, like those they put on the carriage horses in Central Park. Keeps you on track.

Skies are blue, with hardly any clouds. It's been like this for the whole expo. Hopefully only more sun to come.

Cara once again offers little or no information today. No one mentions boarding school, which Lindsay warned me about when I got my first psych eval. And there's no mention of Golan's possible departure to Israel.

Status quo inside Wolf's Den today on property. No disruptions or upsets.

Lindsay became a Hawk this morning, so she should be leaving soon. This reality hits me quite hard, since Lindsay has been my only real friend here. Lindsay is the only other girl here who's my age, 17; the rest are younger. After ALE, she's going to a school/pre-college facility for kids 18 and over. Soon enough I'll be able to visit her in her program in Bend, Oregon. Her program allows cigarettes, probably the only way the kids there can deal with the rest of their torture.

Had Lindsay been offered a choice, she would have chosen going home.

Day 23

The parents of both Lindsay and Christine show up today for their final family meetings before graduation. I'm happy for Lindsay and Christine that they get to graduate, and sleep in a bed, even though I don't. But it's difficult to lose Linds. Watching them reunite with their parents and be filled with excitement about what's to come only reminds me of my reality that I'm still here, and that I have no plans beyond getting through today.

Lindsay reappears after meeting with her parents, smiling from ear to ear. I smile back at her as I turn slowly away so she can't see the tears that start to come, as the dagger is driven into my chest.

Cara has started giving me books to read because I'm finishing the other assignments and they still haven't put me on MOB to Wolf (Mask of Black). I finished the three books, all dealing with self-help, bullying, and similar subjects, so now I'm just plain bored. Lindsay and Christine's Wolf phase lasted for only one expo, so if I get my MOB by the time we leave on the next expo, I could possibly go home within a week or two.

Five more days till Day 28.

Day 24

No morning call today.

The sun is high and everyone is in good spirits. It's a good day for a graduation ceremony, a double one at that. Both Lindsay and Christine are leaving. They're not going home, but to further rehabilitation, and that's because the Adirondack Leadership Expedition specialists don't think it's advisable for either one of them to return home.

Lindsay is off to the better program, I think, far away in Bend, Oregon. It's designed for older teens about to turn 18. There's less supervision and there are more privileges: cigarette smoking is allowed; kids can have off-campus weekends; and everyone gets an allowance. These stipends are unheard-of in therapeutic programs, but the age of the students makes cash allowances advantageous. To be realistic, it's difficult to contain kids that age against their will, considering that they have the legal right to say "Fuck off!" and get the hell out of there.

Christine's program does not sound as promising. Even though she's stuck with the shittier program, she's boasting about how elated she is to be anywhere but here. She's only 16, nowhere near old enough to sign herself out of any facility. She's heading to Bromley Brook School in Manchester Center, Vermont, a therapeutic boarding school for teenage girls who aren't coping in traditional schools. This school is owned by Aspen Educational Group, which also owns ALE. I'm not sure who owns Lindsay's program in Bend (over), Oregon.

On paper, the place sounds great. The brochure for BB looks appealing for a 16-year-old with no other options. All the girls in the pictures are doing some sort of arts and crafts projects, smiling and looking happy. Christine's only request is to be able to ride horses; that's her only passion, besides her big black boyfriends. Bromley Brooke provides horses, but no black men. She's disappointed about the all-girls part, but her parents are certainly more at ease. Her sex life will be at ease too.

As for Lindsay, she's just accepting that she's not allowed to come home after ALE. Because her heroin addiction led her to the wilderness in the first place, her parents don't want to put her back in the same tempting environment as before. Which makes sense. Heroin addiction is not something to play with lightly or take chances with. Lindsay knows that, regardless of how much she wants to go home.

The graduation ceremony isn't at our current campsite, but it's not too far away, so we're not moving camps. Lindsay and Christine fully pack all their gear and take down their tarps. Lucky girls, they're not going to sleep under them anymore. They throw their packs over their backs for the last time and get in line with the rest of the group to hike to the secret location. Secret just means that no FI (future information) is provided.

In formation, we trek out of Wolf's Den past the infirm building and along a cleared dirt road about a quarter mile north to a large open area. Beside the vast open space are four benches surrounding a fire pit. Pete, Allison, and Mike lead us over to the benches.

"Take a seat and spread out, girls. Lindsay and Christine's parents will be arriving shortly."

Not one minute later, a massive black suburban chugs up the dirt path, stirring up dust, and stops a few yards from the benches. All four car doors open, and out come the legs of their parents, followed by the rest of their bodies emerging from the vehicle, smiling widely at their daughters.

The girls run excitedly to their parents with open arms. It's ironic to see them so happy to be with their families after all the horrible things I've heard both of them say about them and their home situations. But their happiness is contagious, and I can't help smiling after them as I watch with just a twinge of jealousy.

The ceremony consists of each girl showing off her skills. Christine demonstrates setting traps and sparking fires. Lindsay does her bow drilling. That's in the phase of Wolf when you have to get a fire started. You create a bow and a spindle, add a top rock to hold the spindle in place, and then set up a cedar board to drill into. Once you have all that, you place the spindle in the string of the bow and work it back and forth fast until it creates heat and sparks into a coal.

Both girls say a few words about their experience and what they learned and are taking home from the program. They're not nervous at all, but look happy and relieved to be leaving.

All four parents are smiling along with their daughters, truly believing that this is the start of better days. (I can practically hear them thinking—they have fixed their child, and now they are embracing their next program of recovery with open arms. What a day to celebrate.)

Christine and Lindsay go around giving last hugs to the other girls and the staff and saying their final goodbyes. It's time for them to go, and a wave of distress and anxiety flows over me. My only connection here has been Lindsay, and now she's leaving. Four more days to Day 28, and I'm not even a Wolf yet. God knows how much longer I have to go.

Thoughts keep filling my mind about what I will say and do at my own graduation ceremony, and I wonder if any of my friends will be allowed to come see me graduate. Christine's sister is here to support her. Because I don't have a sister, could Megan count as a sister? I wonder. Fantasize.

Snapped back to reality, I hug Lindsay when she comes to me last to say goodbye. She takes my journal out of my hands and scribbles down all her information on a blank page.

"You better not lose this, Marissa!" she says. I'm afraid to look her in the eye in case she's about to cry. "This is valuable information on how to contact me once you're out of here. And I am definitely expecting a phone call!"

I don't know it now, but it will take me five years before I finally call her.

The instructors are letting us be for now. Tears start to well up behind my eyes. With all my might, I try hard to hold back the dam until Lindsay gets in the car. This is truly her day and I don't want to do anything to spoil it and upset her. She is my friend; over here, she is, at least.

"I swear I won't lose it," I promise her. "And I'll call you the second I can. Try to enjoy Oregon."

"I will."

"It might not be as bad as you think. Plus you're almost 18. Only a few months more." I wink at her. We both know that once we turn 18, neither of us will be dealing with this bullshit anymore.

"Love you, Marissa." There's a catch in her voice. "You can get through this. If I can, so can you."

"Love you too, Linds. Congratulations. See you in another chapter of our lives."

She gets in the car and I watch the black suburban chug up the dirt road. I wonder if I'll ever see her again.

Now they're gone.

Day 25

Hearing the rustling of dirt and dead leaves, I peek out from inside my tarp. Sarah, our previous instructor who got reassigned to the group, is hurrying over with what looks like coals in her hand. She kneels down next to my tarp and holds out the coals for me to see.

"It's time for MOB!" She smiles at me.

"MOB" means Mask of Black, which is meant to mark you so that everyone knows you're going through transition.

"Finally." I sigh and give her a big sarcastic smile back. I've been waiting days for this.

"Hand me your Nalgene." She motions to my bottle.

Sprinkling a few drops of water onto the crushed coals, Sarah mixes a black paste that she finger-paints all over my face in tribal markings. I'm curious to see exactly how I look right now, but there are no mirrors anywhere, so my face remains a mystery. Sarah finishes painting and sits back on her heels to admire her artistic creation.

"I'm putting Kassandra on MOB as well," she says. "And then I'm calling for everyone to come to the group trap for breakfast. Remember, you're on MOB," she warns me. "So you can't talk to anyone in the group; you can only observe everyone. Also, no talking to Kassandra! You're both on MOB and you're supposed to be ghosts."

Moments of happiness are rare around here. "OK, OK," I agree excitedly.

MOB usually doesn't last more than a day or two, and it has its perks. For one, I don't have to make goals to get spices at dinnertime. No carrying any extra group gear, which is very helpful for the hikes. I don't have to be bothered by speaking to anyone. And it's mandatory for me to write down my opinions on the progress of each individual in the group, which is always fun for me because I am extremely opinionated anyway. Usually my opinion gets me in trouble. Right now it is encouraged. Especially after last week's TC (truth circle) that was all about Marissa and what's wrong with her...

Soon enough, the rest of the girls scurry over to the group tarp and plop down.

"Finally on MOB!" Caroline exclaims, smiling at Kassandra and me.

"It took you guys long enough," Camille says. "I'm already a Wolf and I got here a day after you, Marissa."

Glad that I'm not allowed to reply, I roll my eyes at her. That backhanded compliment is obnoxious. I try not to look bothered, and just walk away with Kassandra.

Camille came to the group one day after me, right after I got out of base camp. She looks nicer than she is—tall and lanky, very skinny, with a pretty face. She has never once smiled at me, and she developed an extreme dislike for me after Raquel and I had our squabble by the water. Worse still, she incites the others against me, and they keep repeating that I'm talking down to them. But it's not *what* I'm saying that bugs them; it's *how* I'm saying it. They all chant that complaint over and over—the girls, the instructors, and even

Cara. Camille and Caroline are butt buddies, and Camille barely talks to anyone else.

Breakfast is as usual, except for my current muteness. By this point in the game, I've picked up a few tricks of the trade from Lindsay about the oats we have to eat every morning. The requirement is one full cup of oats. The oats are raw, with no sugar, no additives, nothing. Straight grain. We are, however, allowed to add a few ingredients to make this meal palatable. In our bear bags we have the choice of dried fruit (gorp), one pack of Swiss Miss hot chocolate mix (to last a week), and about a quarter to a half cup of brown sugar. There's powdered milk for the group as well.

The trick is to fill your cup with as much dried fruit as possible; the bigger, bulkier pieces of course. We're supplied with mainly raisins and dried banana chips, which I hate, yet have learned to tolerate out of hunger and also disgust of raw oats. On occasion, they provide mango chunks and papaya and some unidentifiable items. You fill your cup halfway with this dried fruit and top that with as small a layer of oats as possible. On top of that, you add some sugar, cocoa, and powdered milk. If this isn't enough to fill your cup, you add another very thin layer of oats, then some hot water, and you're done.

This concoction tastes pretty good to me, especially at the beginning of the week when we get new food bags with plenty of sugar and cocoa mix for flavor. You have to be careful to save up, because by the end of the week, you'll be forced to fill up your cup with just those raw oats if you don't have anything else.

Another perk of being on MOB is getting excused from morning and night calls because you're not technically a speaking or active member of the group. You don't have any group obligations.

"Everyone up," Sarah shrieks. "Today is going to be great!" she says as she dances through the campsite.

Our glorified babysitter (i.e., instructor) rounds up the cattle and we're on our way out to expo again.

Day 26

Even though I hate Sarah, who got reassigned to our group yesterday, she's compensating for her lack of sympathy by bringing Shadow, her Golden Labrador retriever. Shadow is simply a great dog—calm, not loud, and adorable. He follows us along and even has his own little pack swung over his back like a saddle. He's a super hiker too; the lucky guy has four feet. It's motivating to have a real live pet around, and it gives us something to play with besides rocks and sticks.

Kassandra and I are especially bored because we're still on MOB and we're not allowed to do anything. We're having problems not talking to each other. Deprived of words, we're communicating through body language.

Undercover notes have started being passed around. This is obviously forbidden, or so we think... it has to be! We're not even allowed to talk to each other out of earshot of our instructors, so we imagine that secret notes must be an even bigger no-no. Our covert actions are probably holding us on MOB longer.

It seems like everyone who joined the group after me has either caught up with my progress or surpassed me. Camille is already a Wolf, and she arrived a day later than I did. And

Kassandra, who's on MOB to Wolf with me, got to ALE a full week or so after I did.

My 28-day plan seems to be backfiring. Even though I've completed all my hard skills before everyone else and better than them, too, the instructors and Cara keep repeating, "You need to work on your soft skills, Marissa. Like your personal growth. Taking accountability, becoming a better you."

I so badly want to respond with a fuck-you finger right in their faces. But I have to hold it in. My program depends on it. Self-control is more important than letting it out. Or so I think.

Some special MOB observations:

Not being allowed to talk makes you think more, and I've been thinking that certain things Raquel does make people lose sympathy for her.

When five other girls in your group have to drink the shit water to clean our cups because we have to be "environmentally conscious," you have to do it, too. You don't get a special "Raquel's retarded so it's OK" pass. Part of the reason for her problems is that people always make excuses for her.

If I could, I'd tell her, "We are all in this same shitty fucked-up boat and everyone has to pull her own weight. Including you. So get with the picture. Stop tossing the remains of your nasty-ass cup on the ground and sliding dirt over it with your foot, hoping that no one sees. Stop sneaking cheese down your pants from lunch so you can add it to your dinner. We know you suck and can't make goals to get spices in your dinner, but you can't cheat your way to getting extra. We all see you! What you are doing is not a bright idea."

There's a new girl in the group, Sam, who's short and fat and looks angry. Her pale skin contrasts with the neon-pink and purple streaks in her short hair. She doesn't want to speak to any of us, which is understandable; I guess that's part of her denial. I assume she knows why she's here, and she's not complaining about it. Most of her attention goes to the dog, which is an escapist way of dealing with things.

Sam stomped her way into our camp the day I went on MOB, so even if I wanted to get to know her, I was not allowed to speak to her. By her appearance even under all the ALE clothing, it's clear why her parents probably didn't understand her type of lashing out. There must be ten holes just in her ears where all her earrings must have been. With her smudged eyeliner and chipped black nail polish, it's obvious that Sam is a bit rough around the edges, to say the least.

Camille has been cracking. And as a result, the formerly sweet, calm, quiet Camille has become angry, aggrieved, and obnoxious. Her passive-aggressive stance is now making *me* angry. I resent her for ripping things from my hands when she wants them because she knows I'm not allowed to respond. And she's laughing and cackling, within earshot, about me with Caroline like an elementary-school girl.

As for Caroline, she's a spunky, tomboyish 14-year-old alcoholic from a town in upstate New York where they have childcare facilities built into their high school for all the teen mothers. What an example. No wonder Caroline was led to alcohol. She used to scare the shit out of her parents when she had boys sleep over at the house and they'd find her stumbling around, drunk, in the backyard at four in the morning, all at the ripe age of 13 and 14 years old.

Being in this particular group of girls feels like regressing to middle school, which is logical, since most of these girls have just recently left middle school.

Something seems off with Sarah this week. It's truly a treat for us that she's brought Shadow along with her, but something seems to be bothering her, aside from the group's overall dysfunction. I can't pry because I'm technically not here. Her personality has changed since the last time she was here, and she's aloof from the group. I don't know how to react to her. I guess she's got her own problems too.

Day 28

Today is my 28th day. The day on which I intended to get in a car and go home.

When they woke me up today, I knew something was different because they blindfolded me, spun me around in three circles, and sent me off to locate the sound of clanking pots and pans. "Go!" they called out.

This is a fun kind of exercise, a sort of rite of passage before becoming a Wolf. Maybe they want us to have occasional carefree feelings.

It's an uphill battle to find the point where the noise is coming from. I'm tripping over rocks and branches that I didn't know were there, and I go flying face-first into the ground. Up again, down again, this goes on for five minutes until I hear the pots and pans right beside me. Grasping at air, reaching around in circles, I desperately grab at the sound. Wham, my hand slams right into the rim of the pot Camille is banging on.

Ripping off the sash around my eyes reveals all the girls in a circle around me, smiling at me. This is motivational and it's also comforting because now I'm one step closer to going home.

What I'm suffering from is a lack of information. All

of my unanswered thoughts are still swirling through my mind. Conversations that should have taken place have been avoided, such as, what's going to happen next? No one has mentioned where I'm going after this.

The night I was taken, I was told that I'd be coming home in 28 days. But here I am on day 28 in the middle of the woods, far from where that promise was meant to take me.

Lindsay and Christine both graduated from the program just days after becoming Wolves. Neither went home, but at least they left ALE. Cara has yet to give me any indication one way or the other. Naturally, I ask every time I see her, but her response is always the same:

"I haven't discussed that with your parents yet, Marissa." Noncommital.

I feel like lecturing her: "How, being my therapist, the therapist to a 'troubled teen,' can you sit so calmly and lie to me? Please don't treat me like the fool you make me out to be. At almost 18 years of age, I have the right to know where I am going and what is coming next for me. You urge us to be honest with you and to take accountability for our actions. You want us to change for the better and see the light of a new day. The mother who bore me, who signed my rights away to these people, promised I'd be home today. If a mother's promise is worth nothing anymore, then what's next for me?"

But I can't say any of that. I can't do anything that might keep me here longer.

I don't sit and cry about it, but I think a lot, analyzing what I'm possibly doing wrong, or what I'm not doing that I should be doing. What's wrong with me, and what's not being fixed? It's crunch time and I need to figure this out. All of my physical skills have been accomplished. They think that's all I'm focusing on, but that's not true. I let it all run through my head, trying to see what I'm doing wrong.

Now that my blindfold is off—at least, the cloth one over

my eyes—I flash one huge fake smile at all the girls, doing what's expected of me.

"Congrats Maris, you're finally a Wolf!" Sarah screeches.

I could do without that "finally." The dog starts to bark as everyone rushes over for a high-five.

"You've really been making some awesome progress," Sarah says, giving me one strong pat on the back.

I'm a Wolf. Now what happens?

Today starts a week of hope.

I've calculated to the best of my knowledge how much time I think I have left here. Generally, becoming a Wolf is the last stage of a student's program. Lindsay and Christine became Wolves a week or two before graduating.

Hawk is the last stage of transition, but Christine never even made it to Hawk, and Lindsay was a Hawk for only one day before graduating.

I predict that at the rate I'm going and the progress I'm making, I should graduate in less than two weeks, or two expos from now. Max.

The most difficult part of becoming a Wolf is bow drilling, which involves several steps: Creating a coal of fire from a wooden, handmade bow, a spindle, and a board of cedar. Drilling the spindle into the cedar with the bow and creating a dark dust called punk, which, if done correctly, turns into a small red ball of fire.

First, you have to find a cedar board somewhere in the woods that's nearly flat and perfect to drill into. Sanding down the spindle into a double-sided stake is similar to the ones I used to pretend to make at summer camp when I went through my "Buffy the Vampire" stage. The top rock that holds the spindle in place is, in my opinion, the most difficult part to make. You have to find a medium-size chunk of wood that preferably isn't cedar, so you don't drill into it as you're drilling down, and you also have to carve a small concave semicircle in the top that perfectly fits your spindle. This way, you get leverage as you push down on the spindle, locking the top rock into place, which keeps it from spinning out of your bow when you push down as hard as you can while ripping the bow back and forth with your other arm.

Actually sparking the coal is not the goal. Practicing for 30 minutes is the goal. It's just a form of busywork. Neither Lindsay nor Christine sparked shit.

Day 30

For this particular week, I'm on my A game. I'm putting personal pride aside and swallowing my words when necessary to avoid problematic drama.

With one truth circle behind me, in which all the girls bashed me, I am not looking to interact with anyone unless I have to. Do my shit, and get the hell out of Dodge, instead of being subjected to middle-school bullshit of who likes who more. I'm sure my parents didn't send me here to make friends.

I've come to the conclusion that no one should be concerned with anyone but themselves while we're all stuck out here. It sounds selfish, but it's true. These girls love to create distractions. But we all need to focus on ourselves and our own growth; otherwise, we're locked into an extended playgroup in the wilderness while our parents get a vacation from us.

Day 31

My body pulses with excitement and anxiety. I am so close to home, I can almost feel it.

All I have left to do is to bust a coal for my TFG (Transfer for Growth) to Hawk. I bow drill day in and day out. On PT, and work time. The burning sensation in my arms is almost debilitating. Except that all I can taste is that fire, that fire that will set me free. Pain is only something that the mind exaggerates.

Tunnel vision until this ends. I'm on a roll and there's nothing stopping me.

Day 32

Expo. Allison and Pete are back. One gift from God. Nice people. There's a third instructor with them, Mike. His energy seems good for the group. His sarcasm doesn't.

Waiting for info.

Caroline, Camille, Kassandra, and I are Wolves together, so it's nice to be able to bow drill with someone for motivation. We are all so close to graduating and have worked extremely hard. I wonder who will become Hawks at the same time.

Fourteen-year-old Caroline's alcoholic personality has been difficult to deal with. But she means well. She's just young and has a lot of free time on her hands, and extra energy that she's trying to subdue.

Caroline's trademark was getting drunk and throwing house parties in her back yard while her parents were asleep in their bedroom. This is what kids do in rural upstate New York, not just cow tipping. Which, by the way, is a real activity that kids engage in, A LOT.

Kassandra's trademark was doing anything and everything under the sun, because she didn't care. Bored with life, Kass turned to drugs and older boys to make life seem easier to live in her not-so-nice neighborhood.

Camille, I've never been so sure about. She did a lot of blow (cocaine), but she's overall nasty. She's quiet and observant, and also smarter than she pretends to be. She knows what she's doing. If she is so calculated, my question is, how did she upset her parents enough for them to decide to send her away.

Caroline will be going to a specialized sports boarding school after here. It'll be good for her. She can direct her liveliness at the soccer ball instead. Kassandra is going to a boarding school, but we don't know which one yet. Camille is going home. No one knows where I am going.

Day 34

Waking up to a burnt walking stick is rather emotionally threatening for me. Most jabs at feelings of security are threatening during these turbulent times.

Your walking stick is one of the first things you are required to make here. Not only does it help you hike, but it symbolizes your stability. It's your personal symbol of strength to carry you through this strenuous program.

Mike walks up next to me and looks down at the ashes in the fire pit, in which only the top handle of my staff remains. The rest of it burnt up. How did it get in the fire pit?

We stand here for a second while it sinks in that my walking stick is gone. Internally, I collapse. It's so crushing to see that everything I've worked for in the past 34 days has burned beyond repair. A tear rolls down my cheek.

"Oh, yeah, you left that out by the fire last night," Mike says. "So I threw it in the fire because you forgot to bring it to your tent." He sounds so casual.

Smack, right to my chest.

I slowly turn my head and look him in the eye. "You did what?" I ask coldly.

"I threw it in the fire. You aren't supposed to forget your personal belongings."

"You're a real piece of shit," I tell him matter of factly.

"I think that warrants five alternative words other than shit, Marissa," he retorts.

In this very moment, everything that has been bottled up into a perfect little package of productivity and positivity is gone. My vision is blurred by tears, and my chest gives in from the pain.

"You can go fuck yourself," is my only offer to his request. I turn away from Mike and walk to the farthest edge of camp that I can.

Mike starts following me, but Pete grabs him by the arm. "Let her go," he says.

Later in the day, Caroline becomes a Hawk. I do not.

Back at property, Cara comes by with two new girls for our group: Sarah and Erin. Sarah is 17 and she's a wild child from Long Island who drives a Beemer (BMW). At least now I have someone my age.

Erin, who's 15, has social problems and is all-around awkward. I feel a sad, sorry twinge of compassion for this girl who looks as if she just doesn't know how to fit in. No one has the patience to talk to her, not even the instructors most of the time. I have nothing better to do, so I'm talking to her.

Cara gave me photos of my parents and me today, but didn't meet with me. She has decided to camp with us tonight.

Something is wrong. Very wrong.

Day 36

"Marissa, you're up! Time to talk," Cara says with her usual insincere smile.

Uncurling myself from my Indian-style seat on the ground by the fire, I make my way toward Cara. Just out of earshot of the group, we sit facing each other on the ground. She smiles sympathetically.

"So I heard what happened with Mike and the walking stick," she begins.

I'm getting a bad feeling about this conversation already. "Yeah, he burned it and I was pissed. Sorry for cursing at him." I want to explain this to her, but she cuts in before I can say anything more.

"It's OK. But I have some difficult news that I need to share with you. Well, that your parents need to share with you." She digs into her manila folder and pulls out a letter from my parents.

My heart starts to thump and I'm breaking into a cold sweat. I start to read. Most of the letter is a blur, but what catches my attention is the only thing I need to know:

"We are so sorry, Marissa. But after speaking with Cara and discussing this between ourselves, we feel it best that you do not come home after your stay in ALE."

This is the sentence that will change my life forever.

A hot flash with a wave of losses comes over me. Disappointment. Betrayal. Rejection. Anger. Helplessness.

I used to have a strong sense of what my future was going to look like. I was going to go to college in California. I was going to have a bright career that moved a lot of people, with whatever industry I decided to go into. I was most likely going to continue my career out in L.A., and I was going to be happy. None of these aspirations were inconsistent with the objective facts of my life.

The light that I so clearly saw at the end of the tunnel has now dimmed to black. I open my mouth to speak, but no words come out. It's like I'm having a stroke. I'm paralyzed, immobilized.

In a split second I see everything I had built my entire life to be, ripped out right from under me. Flashback to the night when I was taken from my room… the look in everyone's eyes around me… my mother assuring me that what she believed was right… my father barely able to look at me at all.

Never did I think I would feel so abandoned, forsaken by the only people in the world who should love and protect me. If they don't, who will?

Right now, in this second, with this letter, I feel worse, far worse, than I did even on that night when I was jolted out of a deep sleep and driven away. All along, I've believed—I *had* to believe—that there was an endpoint to this imprisonment, this torture that seems to have no goal. From the moment I stepped inside the car that drove me here, I've been looking forward to proving myself and getting the hell out of here.

No. It's not to be. There is no end to the program. There is no light at the end of the tunnel. With the stroke of a pen, my parents have sacrificed the rest of my adolescence to a corporation meant to institutionalize and rehabilitate teenagers.

Am I really being institutionalized just for growing up and joining in on the fun of being in high school? Where, by the way, I was never even invited to any "cool kid" parties until my junior year? This reign of uncontrollable behavior, which my parents so strongly believe I am here for, lasted all of a school year, until they decided to fix me, right before finals even started.

I am 17 years old. It is August, and I turn 18 in February. Six months from now, I'll be allowed my legal right to freedom again. I will never again be under my parents' rule. I will no longer be a minor.

But until that day of freedom, months away, my parents have sold me out to someone else. Or rather, something else. An institution.

That night when I was being taken, I sat upright in my bed, looked my mother in the eye, and told her, "This will change everything forever." I didn't know how drastically it would radically transform my life. I definitely did not think I'd never be living home at again. Home is now only a distant memory.

Cara tells me matter-of-factly that they still have not chosen a school for me. My program has just turned into a waiting game.

Day 37

Absorbing myself in helping Erin transition seems to be the thing to do for me. It puts on a front that I am progressing and being a strong leader to the odd girl out, and it's distracting me from the harsh reality of seeing no end to this jail sentence. There is nothing else to absorb myself in besides Erin. There is nothing I can do for myself any longer.

My focus has switched from "I can't wait to go home to my friends and family" to "If only I can get out of here to sleep on a bed and be indoors."

Cara tries in her own inadequate way to comfort me. An educational consultant is coming to meet with me to properly place me in the correct school, she promises.

From that letter, Cara says, it seems that my parents want something with minimal therapy, where I can still pursue college. If there's a college that will accept me from that kind of high school...

I also had a career. Have a career. I was on Broadway at age eight. My whole life has been consumed by going on auditions and casting calls. Am I now supposed to give that up because everyone thinks I'll be better off in therapy 24/7?

I can't comprehend this discrepancy: the father and mother who used to drive me into Manhattan from suburban

New Jersey every day after school to work at the show are the same people who are now so willing to throw away everything I've worked for. Everything I've been trained to do ever since I was able to learn and follow orders.

I've been in two Broadways shows and multiple commercials, voiceovers, and off-Broadway shows. I've been a member of Screen Actors Guild, Equity, and Aftra since age nine. Being onstage was who I was. Who am I now? Who do they think I am? And who are they?

I sense that the instructors know I'm having a hard time coping with this news, so they don't expect me to be on top of my game. This allows me some leniency for a day or two, at least until the next expo.

The letter did say something about a possible pre professional school in California. Let's just hope I'm going there and not to some reform school full of misfits. California is a glimmer of hope that I'm now gripping onto.

Back to Erin. Hopefully they'll let me help turn her into a Bear by tomorrow so she can at least talk.

Day 38

Today I'm starting to write goodbye letters to various friends, one of whom, Megan, is my closest. My letter to her starts like this: "You are and always will be my best friend." It rambles on for three pages because I feel like I'm writing my last letter before going off to war, not knowing if I'll ever see her again.

Little do I know . . .

All of my letters sound unreasonably dramatic and depressed. I reread them and decide never to give them to Cara. First of all, she might not even send them to my parents for distribution to my friends. But more than that, the last thing I want is to make them sad, too.

Obviously I've done something wrong here. It's Day 38. I'm still under a tent in the middle of the woods. And today is ten days after my first goal line, Day 28.

I need to go about things differently. Maybe the goal isn't to focus on going home. Maybe I need to focus on the thought process they want me to have in order to get away from here. Being perfect and not showing emotion is also showing them no growth. Blowing up now and then ultimately shows that I've been bottling up bigger emotions.

Is it sobriety they want to see me pledge to? Do they really think that's my problem? Why else wouldn't I be ready to go home? If weekly therapy sessions are all that my parents want from me, then fine, I'll adhere. If they want to drug-test me at this point, I won't even care.

Something tells me that if I'm going to go down, I might as well do it fighting. Let's change the strategy.

I've got a good gig going with the helpfulness—with Erin, Sarah, and also Slammer, one of the new girls. That's her nickname. She's interesting, and she's also resistant. Back home, she went to punk shows and was rebelling against how she was expected to look and behave. Slammer is aggressive, and she lashes out in angry ways.

Becoming a Hawk is just around the corner, what with all my bow drilling and other skills I've done. They have nothing else to do with me when I zip through all the program lessons, busywork, and books to read. They will have to promote me to Hawk.

Sobriety is the new game I'll play. But they'll have to see the transition. They have to see the seed growing in my head and truly believe that I believe it myself. If I can convince the instructors, then maybe the letter I'm going to write to my parents will actually persuade them to let me come home. They haven't made a decision yet, so there's still time.

I wonder if my parents get scanned copies of the letters I actually write, or if Cara retypes them her way and then emails them?

Day 39

The one thing that institutions hate more than anything else is corruption from the inside out. It's the most lethal form. That happens when the group is brainwashed to think and believe a certain way, but there's one person in the bunch who doesn't agree. There's a strong chance that the dissident will spread her thoughts to the others, and in so doing, shed light on what might be a false conception.

These wilderness programs and therapeutic boarding schools thrive on fear. Their representatives give your parents the notion of a model child, and how different you are from that ideal, and what horrible things might happen to you if you don't change course and mend your ways. They falsely assure parents that they can transform their foul-mouthed, pot-smoking, promiscuous, black-clothes-wearing progeny into model children.

In the end, everything is about perception. And if it looks good enough, and what they are selling is persuasive enough, desperate parents will take the offer. That's what mine did.

Day 40

Erin is shooting her mouth off while hiking, talking all about her plans for what she's going to do after ALE.

"Shut the fuck up, Erin," I snap after 20 minutes of this. "You're delusional if you think you're going home after this."

"Why would you say that?" Erin sounds almost sad.

Kassandra joins in: "Because no one goes home after this, and it's a sorry thought to think you are too."

"And you're here at what, 15 years old?" I say. "This is just an easier solution for your family, to handle the trouble without facing it themselves. It's not like we don't understand what you're going through."

Kass and I shoot looks at each other.

"I just miss my friends," Erin says dejectedly.

"So do we," we say in unison.

Later at night I make up for it by convincing Erin that we only tried to show her the harsh reality so in the end it'll be easier for her when that day comes. I feel bad that Erin has blind faith in me and believes I'm saying these things for her own good. That even though I'm breaking inside and having trouble sugar-coating things, I'm still making others feel better. When really, I'm saying all this because I am terribly hurt that my circumstances haven't changed, and that hers still can.

Day 41

A bit more optimistic today on a day hike.

We're at a lean-to for expo, which is great because we didn't have to pitch any tarps last night on this weird swampy ground. We took our day packs, and I didn't pack much besides my journal.

The hike yesterday to get here was full of rain and bushwhacking, but today is bright and clean. The sky is crisp and the grounds are easy hiking, the path cushioned by pine needles on our way up the mountain to the north of our camp.

Sarah yells, "Everyone gather around, we're gonna play a game."

Yeah, Sarah is back.

Great, I think. *What now?*

"We're going to learn to work together as a group. We are going to carry this log up the mountain with us until we reach the summit." She points to a huge log that looks as if it weighs 50 to 60 pounds. Almost the weight of our hiking packs, anyway.

"One person on each side of the log. Carry it up for five minutes, then switch teams. Slammer and Marissa, you're first. Then Kassandra and Erin."

More stupid busywork. I can only imagine Kass's disgust at having to deal with Erin right now on this task. Erin's intentions are never bad; she just doesn't know when to shut up. And she's new, so she won't physically be able to carry this log well, which will make for some great entertainment for me. They always say that the road to Hell is paved with good intentions. I'm starting to understand that more and more now.

When Slammer first got here, she was not my number-one fan. But she and I are quite strong together, and I don't think this will be much of a struggle. If anything, it's a chance for me to show how far I've come physically and in teamwork.

"I feel energized," I announce after we reach the summit. "I imagine I feel this way because our hike with the log was a success. In the future I'd like to continue the good teamwork to have a strong group." I take advantage of this moment to say one of five "I Feel" statements to make goals tonight. There aren't many goals for me to set in order to get spices at dinnertime, since I've finished all the program lessons and hard skills. My three required tasks per day are getting more boring because I have less and less to do.

My other two tasks are to write a letter to my parents discussing my feelings about boarding school, and to finish my bow for bow drilling. I snapped my first bow a couple of days ago while drilling so hard into the board. My walking stick was burned, my bow broke, and I'm not going home. Things are not looking up.

I start my letter but don't get very far:

Mom and Dad,

I'm coping with the news about going to boarding school well . . . . .

Not really . . . .

Day 42

There's a sun shower set up in the trees today. It's a big clear plastic bag filled with gallons of water from the lake, with little openings I've pierced in it to let the water sprinkle out slowly. Gazing at the endless greens lining the mountain, I let the clean raindrops trickle down on me. Not thinking at all, I'm enjoying being naked, taking a shower in the middle of nowhere with fresh open air and sunlight, no dirty walls closing in on me.

I'm certainly starting to get used to living in the woods and being comfortable with it. Even when it rains at night, I'm not afraid. The rain is actually a comforting sound. The different kinds of rain sound like drumsticks beating down on my blue tarp. Each has a different rhythm and sound, depending on how much rain there is and how heavily it's coming down. That's the only music we get out here.

Indoor showers have been a different story, however. My first few experiences with on-property showers have not gone well. These free-standing plastic structures are cramped, enclosed, and disgusting. They're lined up right next to each other, four in a row, inside the infirm, a cement building. The first time, I refused altogether to take a shower, insisting that

I'd end up dirtier than if I just sweltered in my own accumulated oil and dirt.

That's why this sun shower is a gift. I've never taken one before and it's quite liberating during this time of always feeling trapped. I undress quickly, close my eyes, and let the water drip down my face, neck, back, and legs and into the grass beneath my bare feet. Whoosh! Fresh water, open air, no nasty infirm building to clean up afterward. I could stand here for days in this open shower. I can almost see the condensation misting off my overheated body as the cool water soothes my sun-seared skin.

Our days in the woods are always roasting hot, and I constantly feel like I'm burning, except for when I'm sleeping, and then I freeze. Heat sits in my chest throughout the day, mostly because of anxiety and the demands of strenuous hiking. Apart from the heat, the burning sensation is often overwhelming, fed by fear, uncertainty, anger, betrayal, confusion, and planning for something that can't be planned. The loss of my life as I knew it throbs like a knife wound. Standing under this open-sky shower and washing myself clean, I still feel the knife stuck in my heart, exactly where it was thrust the night I was taken, although my body is starting to heal around it.

As calm and peaceful as I feel right now, in this moment, under the sun and clean water from the lake, that knife is still there. And it's not going anywhere.

Keeping my blinders on, I dry off in the sun, still hidden from the group for privacy, but with my legs in sight of the instructors to assure them that I haven't run away. Where's there to go, anyway? I used to think about running during my first few days here. It's not worth it in the end; you'll get caught, or hurt, or lost, and starve to death.

My mind settles back into work mode. Today's self-imposed agenda is to bow drill for 30 minutes and then get through my

Bear pro, which means to review my Bear skills so they know I haven't forgotten anything basic; keeping in mind, at all times, to get the fuck out of here ASAP. I'm already way overdue with my time here.

I've been slowed down because a couple of days ago, Camille stole the top rock for my bow drilling set and it got lost in the woods. I reported her, but no one believed I'd lost it until I made myself a new one. And certainly no one believed that perfect Camille would either take mine or toss it to make my stay harder. She was too nice and sincere for that.

After I master the rest of my skills for Wolf, I can request my TFG to Hawk once we return to property a few days from now. My strategy is to request my transfer first, before Caroline and Camille do, because I've been working harder than anyone else, and I've been showing it, and with a smile on my face, too. My real self does not belong here. So I've invented a new person for them. Maybe it's changing me as well, but right now I can't tell if it's for the better or worse.

Camille always looks smug, as if she has everything under control. She knows she's going home after she's through with ALE, and she acts bitchy and superior because of that. Contrast that with my situation, where I sat in the woods wishing and waiting and working harder than I ever have in my life in order to go home, and then on day 36 I was finally told that I'm going far from home, to some nameless institution. But Camille gets to go home. Her demeanor since she arrived has been impressively calm, with little crying, if any at all. Her voice is low and never aggressive. Mastery of passive aggression is her strong suit, which the instructors don't notice because they're dealing with six other abrasive girls. Camille seems like a saint compared to us because she doesn't question anything. She's a better liar than I am.

I guess my biggest downfall was always telling my parents the truth about where I went and what I did. In retrospect, lying might have worked out better for me in most scenarios. In any case, it didn't matter whether I was honest or not because my parents always assumed that I was lying. Every time I walked into my house from an after-school activity, even if I came home at 8 p.m., my mother would call me into the den to talk.

And then the inspection would begin. She would ask how my day was, and then proceed to smell my breath. Sometimes she would wrongfully accuse me of drinking (which I never did because it made me nauseous before I got to have any fun), or she'd accuse me of being stoned, often when I wasn't. This was not exactly a scientific procedure.

Sometimes I had smoked. But neither drinking nor smoking mattered. My mother wasn't after the truth. The inconsistency of her accusations proved her faulty detective skills and made it clear that she was going to believe whatever she wanted about what I was doing when I wasn't at home.

I'm assuming that I may get one day or even a week at home before my parents ship me off to God knows where. So I smile on, get out of the sun shower, throw my clothes back on, and go back to work on my bow, silently.

Day 43

I start my letter:

> Mom and Dad,
> I'm coping well with the news about going to
> boarding school. I am actually excited about the
> prospect of going to a school in California, believe it
> or not. I want to be able to focus on college and get
> into UCLA early decision. I hope you are considering
> my ideas for schools as well. I have given Cara a list of
> schools some of my acting friends go to in L.A. that
> allow you to continue your career while in school.
> Cara mentioned a minimal-therapy school, so maybe
> could I go to school and therapy separately? I think
> this could potentially be good if I'm placed well...

I read what I've written so far and decide that these few
short sentences say enough. I am actually feeling excited about
the possibility of going to a school in California because I
want to go to college there anyway. Of course, this letter
sounds overly enthusiastic, but everyone's just so conspicuously happy and chipper around here all the time, so let's play

along. I may be upset about not having my senior year, but I'd be thrilled to go to an acting school.

We return to property after expo and I meet with Ben Mason, the boarding school consultant who helps families properly place their children in school after their wilderness experience. Ben names a lot of schools, rattling off various pros and cons for each. I'm not getting a sense of where he's leaning, but I'm trying to push him in the only direction that sounds like a good one to me—to California. My entire life once mapped out to a California destination, so it seems like a jumpstart to get there a year before college starts. Plus, I'll be a California resident if I go to school there, facilitating my University of California application. But this meeting, like most around here, ends without a conclusion.

Keeping my arm strong with my bow, I keep on bow drilling while contemplating where I may or may not be sent.

Graduation.

Not mine.

Camille's. She and Caroline are graduating on the same day.

I've hated Camille, the bitch, since three days ago, when the top rock for my bow drilling set mysteriously went missing during our last expo. I suspected her and asked if she'd seen it.

"Oh no, Marissa," she protested. "You must have just dropped it during a hike or something."

That's all she had to offer, while I feverishly looked everywhere around camp for my rock to bow drill with. Ripping apart my personal belongings, over and over. Asking everyone around camp if they had seen it. Nowhere.

"Camille, I know I had it here," I told her, after half an hour of searching, knowing exactly where I'd left it. She's good at lying. She's the mean girl from Charleston, South Carolina who did a lot of cocaine, ran with the "cool girls," and perfected the art of passive aggression before she ended up here.

"I did not drop it anywhere; I am more than careful with my things, especially since Mike torched my entire walking stick. I know you took it."

"No, I would never do anything like that. Why would I jeopardize the fact that I am going home so soon?" She smiled coyly back at me.

"You don't see it as jeopardizing anything because you're still going home, and you kiss everyone's ass, and you've been seen as perfect since you got here. You don't care about anything anymore, certainly not me. Maybe Caroline, but I wonder how long that friendship will last outside ALE. You're conniving, and you know it, and you're happy you pulled one over on me."

She showed no remorse and smiled innocently, aware that I knew the truth but couldn't touch her—she was invincible.

She smiled silently at me. Infuriating. Shrugging her shoulder, she did a quick turn that whipped her long hair around her shoulders. "Guess you'll never know, then," she hissed and glided away.

But I will know, and I *do* know. Her graduation is already going on and it's too late to do anything about it. Her sidekick, Caroline, hyperactive but goodhearted, just admitted what happened. The day my top rock disappeared, Camille got Caroline to swipe it while I wasn't looking. Then Camille grabbed it from her and threw it into the woods. Caroline was afraid to say anything before today. Camille is her best friend here, she explained, and she didn't want to upset anyone during her last week.

Now Caroline and Camille are graduating in spite of it all.

I remember Camille's first day at camp pretty vividly. She arrived just before Lindsay and Christine graduated. She looked emaciated and in need of a hamburger, but was pretty and reserved and seemed like someone who might become a friend. I really needed a new friend now that Lindsay was gone, and I sincerely hoped Camille would fill that role.

The way it turned out, our personalities were not a good

mix. Maybe she wasn't there to make any connections, except to Caroline, who became her butt buddy. It hurt me not to have anyone with whom I could identify, at least until Kassandra joined the group three weeks later.

Now Kass and I are sitting together, watching Camille graduate and head back to South Carolina, back to her home, friends, and family. No one can stop her now.

At this point, more than six weeks into my involuntary adventure, everyone's graduation is sort of a slap in the face. I've been in the woods for 44 days now, and I've been back on property, and I've been a Wolf for one week. I have now finished all my skills and I'm requesting my TFG to Hawk so I can go home. But when am I going home? Tomorrow? Before our next expo? Will I have to go off property yet again and deal with still more bushwhacking and bullshit busywork until the therapists, the school consultants, and my parents all decide where to put me?

After this latest graduation is over, Cara comes by for her weekly drop-in. Which doesn't seem much like therapy anymore; it's more like news-bearing. She meets with Raquel, who comes back bouncing, whispering that Cara "pretty much told her" that the three of us are going to get to graduate together next week. So it looks like one more expo for Raquel, Kass, and me.

OK, I can handle that. One last expo, one last week. Now all I have to do is get through MOB (Mask of Black) for Hawk, then do some work for Hawk, and by the time we are back on property, it should be smooth sailing.

I'm writing to my parents again and again, trying to convey the message that I'm willing to go to whichever pre-professional school they want to put me in, as long as they don't stick me in a lockdown. A therapeutic boarding school with no music program wouldn't be ideal for a child they once considered enrolling in a Montessori school.

Till now, I've always thought I knew my parents. Or at least had a relationship with them where we could discuss things openly. I prided myself on not lying, ever. Never pushed curfew, was always on time and where I needed to be, when I needed to be. My mom would always call me the minute my curfew ended. I would simply walk through the door smiling instead of answering the phone.

Being thrown into a wilderness program seemed wacky and out of character for them to begin with. Following that with boarding school for my senior year is incomprehensible. Every notion I once had about my parents is being chipped away, day by day. From one decision to another, they are completely foreign to me now. Who *are* these two, and why are they doing these things to me—in effect, exiling me? If I go to boarding school for my last year of being a minor, and then go off to college, their only child will never live at home with them again.

My only hope is to have a couple of my best friends, really only two, come attend my graduation, even if they get sent home right after. Golan, who's going into the Israeli Army, and my best friend Megan. All of my letters to Megan and Golan have sounded like permanent goodbye letters. Golan leaves for Israel before the new school year. And then he's moving to Israel forever. This is my last-ditch effort to get to see him at all. Everything was ripped from me so suddenly. Don't I get a tiny bit of a break? One face-to-face visit with two people who matter more to me than anyone else in the world right now, before I get shipped away to yet another institution?

Grasping at air.

Day 45

"Pack up, girls, we're moving."

Expo? I think, confused. Today is the day we're supposed to leave.

"Everything like normal, no trace left behind, and water run before we get going," the instructors recite drearily, as they do every morning.

OK. I grab my tent down, fold all my stuff, shove it in my bag, and...

"Marissa," Slammer calls from across camp, "I don't have time to do the water run. Can you do it for me so we can get out of here on time?"

"For sure," I answer, smiling at her in spite of being stressed. I have my own tent to break down, the team tarp to break down, and now Slammer's tasks. If we don't break down camp in our allotted time today, I don't get to request my TFG to Hawk because we would miss one of our calls. The group has to make five in a row collectively before anyone can request to move levels. It's a way of keeping us working together as a group and in sync. This rule applies throughout the entire program, not just to one set of five. When new members come in, or if one person is having a bad week, that could potentially postpone someone's entire program. We're living the epitome of a perfect commune. Communism. Following Marx's rules at all times.

I throw all my shit into my pack, which is not packed as neatly as I would like for the hike. If you don't pack tightly and in order, it's harder to hike because the weight isn't distributed properly. I run down to the water station to fill up at least ten Nalgenes of water. Filling up gallons upon gallons of water is never the quickest task. And water is not air. It's heavy! Carrying ten Nalgenes is a workout. Plus, to get to this particular water spigot, you have to go through some trees and down a hill. Climbing back up with full Nalgenes is strenuous. There's no time for dropping any of them by accident. And you certainly can't leave any behind if you do drop one. Someone will notice, and even if we've hiked all the way to our next location, we'll have to hike all the way back for just one water bottle.

I race back up to camp and slide into line with the other girls right on time.

"Call," screams one of the instructors. "You guys made it. Good job! Looked like it was going to be a close one, Marissa. We were waiting for you."

I laugh sarcastically, smirk, and step forward to say, "Um, hey guys, I'm requesting my TFG to Hawk now. We have our five calls in a row. Thanks." I smile at them.

Everyone looks at me, and I return their stares with a deadpan expression.

Kassandra goes on MOB. I do not. One by one, my friends are moving up and graduating.

Yesterday's hike took us from one end of property to another. Strange. I thought for sure we would have an instructor changeover, leave property, and go out into the woods. Especially since Camille and Caroline have graduated, we have no business remaining on property.

"Make a day pack, girls. We're going on a day hike."

Again, strange. Out of order for the program's stringency. OK. We're staying on property at a great location, Bear's Den, which I particularly like because of its level ground. It's easy to pitch your tarp, and the flat ground is much more comfortable than at off-property sites. Bear's Den is better than the other on-property sites as well. The ground is dry and not rocky or slanted, and the trees are positioned in an intricate maze, allowing for convenient placement of our tarps. We can be close to each other and whisper through our tents at night, which isn't possible on rough terrain.

Late-night talks have been one of my few comforts here. The night of July 4, when we camped in woods that were difficult for tarp placement, Lindsay and I were next to each other. We were joking about the size of the blunts we'd be smoking after here, full of the weed that they tell us is ruining our futures. We laughed quietly and reminisced about our friends at home. And we told each other what the instructors call "war stories," meaning that we were glorifying the negative behavior that got us here, like drinking or smoking.

We're teenagers, we do these things, and they're fun and a rite of passage. Lindsay laughed and said, "Well, I'm definitely not going to go home and shoot heroin again, I know that's wrong, but a beer and a blunt sounds just right."

I laughed back and said, "I agree." I really miss Lindsay now.

Now Kass and I get to pitch our tents close together, here at Bear's Den. That helps defeat loneliness for one night, at least. Loneliness is one aspect of living out in the woods. On expo, you're forced to pitch your tarps far from one another because the ground has few acceptable sleeping spots. When you first come to ALE, you often want to be alone, but not when you're so far into your program, as I am right now. You're done with your own recycled thoughts, which drive you crazier by the minute once you reach Day 40.

As we start our day hike, we pass the infirm. The black suburbans that bring us to wherever we're going for the day are not there. We turn onto a familiar path that might lead to Wolf's Den or somewhere near there, but we pass Wolf's Den and keep on hiking. The way these instructors walk us is somewhat like walking a dog. The dog doesn't know where the person is leading it, and the person feels no need to inform the dog.

We don't follow the trail that turns out of the high grass area to Wolf's Den, but continue through the high grass, blindly. Instructors aren't giving us any FI (future information), so we follow like sheep (or dogs) up the hill, and still farther up the hill.

It feels like hours, and we're tiring fast. When you hike

through tall grass and can't see an end or a summit, you feel like you're going nowhere fast. It's different on expos, where your body signals fatigue as you approach campgrounds. After you've been out on a few expos, you can sense the limit; you can predict how much they'll push you for a hike each day.

Day hikes are different because we aren't carrying our normal heavy weight, so we just keep on walking. Silence. Walking. Silence. More tall grass. It's as monotonous as it sounds and far more exhausting.

Finally the grass gets shorter and opens up into a field.

"Time for lunch. Pick a place to sit and eat and think quietly."

We always sit and eat in silence. Nothing new here, guys…

We're high up and about to look out onto the expansive grounds of property; to observe just how much land the company owns for hiding away secret campsites and providing endless acres of woods to wander about in. No wonder it's not the smartest move to run; you would probably run yourself right back to the infirm and get caught.

"Back to camp, guys. Packs on."

And we're back off down the hill to Bear's Den for more arbitrary and meaningless assignments they will have to give us to make up for the time we didn't spend hiking on our usual expo. We have literally just walked through grass for a couple of hours, just to go back to where we came from. No mountains, no tasks, no moving camps. Just silent walking for hours, and only to turn around and walk right back. I really do search for some meaning in what they do, yet they make it so damn hard.

Day 47

Kassandra becomes a Hawk. I am extremely happy for her and love her to death; she's my best friend here. But now I sit back and watch yet another girl who came into the program weeks after I did push past me, and I still don't know what I'm doing wrong. It's an enormously helpless feeling to try over and over, to look at yourself day after day, and yet come up with nothing; still with no idea how to fix the problem that is right in front of you.

I requested my TFG to Hawk two days ago. I have no more skills to accomplish to move past where I am now in the program. So I just keep on bow drilling. It is a somewhat exhausting activity, bowing hard and fast into a cedar block to create fire. But it quiets the mind and lets your thoughts turn into meditation, as opposed to plotting strategies. Bow drilling is a close second to my favorite way of making fire, sparking it off a rock.

I've been suspecting that my parents are the source of this long delay. I'm not sure they know what they want to do with me, and they're probably in a long debate over where to send me after the program. From their point of view, thinking about it for a week is normal. From my point of view, a week in the wilderness feels like a month. Therapists and parents don't talk every day, so decisions get delayed, the process slows down, and you get caught in the middle. I am for sure not the instructors' top priority.

"Staying at Bear's Den," barks an instructor. "Pack a day pack. We're taking a quick detour to the infirm before we leave for expo."

An instructor changeover is going on. "Felt like a lifetime," I whisper to Kassandra. "Thank God Sarah's leaving."

"I like her dog, though," she says.

"Me too, but she's the instructor and the dog is just there to play with. I'll take a new instructor over keeping the silent animal."

Kassandra tilts her head to the side, nods, and then smiles.

Freed from "Sarah's rule," now we see Pete. "Pete!" Kass and I yell and run to him, excited. "Can't believe we got you back again!" I say. "After the last set of instructors, you were needed big time!"

Pete smiles at the warm welcome and gets straight to business. "Time for our day hike. Hop in a car. Let's get going, it may be a long hike."

Back in the suburbans, cars I know well by this point, we drive for a few miles on the highway. Passing a bunch of old stopping-off places I remember from hikes past, still we keep on driving. The highway up here in the Adirondacks is lined with mountain after mountain in different shapes and sizes. They're tall, and shorter; some look like animals, and some resemble various figures. When you don't know your destination, the drive seems like eternity. I used to try to mark the path that the cars took, looking closely at all the turns we made just in case I ever wanted to escape. I stopped playing that game a while ago. My good sense of direction is no match for millions of small streets that all look the same, with no landmarks. I've been here for almost seven weeks.

Forty-five minutes later, all the cars pull over to the base of a mountain called Catamount. It's a ski area with a vertical descent of a thousand feet, and there are loads of ski trails and hiking trails marked by vintage-looking wooden arrow signs pointing in every direction. As far as I can see, the path we will be taking is pretty flat, leading into a thick forest blocking our view. Looking up, you can see the mountain pop out from the trees and tower upward into the sky.

When prepping mentally for a hike, all the girls gather, look up at the mountain, and predict how high, how long, how far, and how hard this hike is going to be.

"Looks pretty doable," Slammer says from behind me.

I turn. "Yeah, maybe an hour hike up?"

Erin looks worried. "Marissa, I'm scared. What if I can't make it up?"

I'm worried too. Erin is weak and small, and she wasn't athletic before coming here. My background in gymnastics and other activities helps me summon the strength and endurance required to survive out here. Erin's got a long way to go in building those muscles. Therefore it means a slower hike for us, and more energy spent to help her make it to the top. But it's all or none. We're not going back to camp till we all make it up.

"That's not an option," I warn her. "Molly stopped hiking on one of my first days here, and then all of a sudden she was ripped from the group and never seen again."

"Oh." Erin looks down at her shoes.

"I'll help you," I promise. "You'll be fine. It's mental. We'll all make it up, and the quicker and harder we hike, the easier it will be to get down, and the more time we'll have to get back to property before the sun goes down."

I will help her, I think to myself. If I'd had some moral support when I first got here, my hikes would have gone much smoother. Instead, I was crying and wasting all my energy on hyperventilating. Focusing on helping Erin will help out the entire group. She's been a bit slow because these are her first hikes, and our group is only as good as our weakest link. Only time will bulk her up. It's not getting any easier.

This mountain is one of the only tourist lures for people visiting the Saranac Lake area. On the way up, we're passing a lot of families and also hikers out for the day. They must think that we're prisoners, all dressed alike in red pants and orange hats. I try not to focus on them or it will just make me anxious that I'm being watched, and most likely judged. Up and up we go. The path is all lined and littered with hikers other than us, which also makes it encouraging. Accustomed to hiking up the sides of mountains that civilians aren't allowed on, seeing all these people struggling up a mountain with us makes us compete to reach the top faster than they do.

Two and half hours later, we arrive at the summit. Two and half hours up a mountain is a long, hard hike.

Generally the program tries to keep us away from civilians so we don't have a way to escape; for example, by somehow getting someone to meet us during a hike. Or while we're eating at the summit, tell a sob story to some civilian who might help us to escape somehow.

But we're a strong, older group at this point, and Erin isn't going to convince anyone of anything, and Slammer looks angry all the time and has weirdly dyed hair. No one is going to help her break free. We're safe in our captivity. Our jumpsuits are clear enough identification to make hikers tug their children closer as we pass.

Now we're headed down. I've always been a fan of obstacle courses. Skipping down a steep mountain creates jumps and leaps, and it tests your agility. Skipping turns the last part of the hike into a potential obstacle course of sorts. It took us forever to climb up the mountain, which always makes the hike down enjoyable and easy because we already know what we're in for and what to expect.

I was right about the first part of the hike being a flat winding path to the base of the mountain. This winding path is covered by thousands of trees everywhere, hiding the intricacies of trails that lead you to the mountain's start point. Maybe they made this part of the hike long enough to scare people not prepared to go uphill before they even start climbing.

Hop, hop, hop, hop, light on my toes and running down the path, I feel lighter on my feet than normal.

Pete starts laughing at me. "You seem to be extra happy today."

I think about this. "Well, we're almost done with the hike, which, although it took forever, went well. Erin's doing better and not complaining as much. Which for me is a great thing, considering that I've tried to take her under my wing, and when she starts whining and making a fuss, the other girls look at me as if I failed. And it didn't rain. It's been a nice cool da....."

SMACK. I fall and land hard on my face.

"Hahahaha, Oh my God, are you okay? Hahaha! That was epic!" Pete rushes over to try to help me up.

"You went flying like Superman," Sam spits out as tears of laughter drip down her face.

"Outstretched, and you got air, and gained ground and everything. That was a great fall, Marissa!" Kassandra chokes out.

The rest of the girls, Erin and Raquel, are laughing too. Raquel probably sees this as retribution for the times I was mean to her.

I pop up and look down at my knee, which is now bleeding. The fall ripped through my red pants and long johns and tore my skin open. "I'm OK," I say, laughing. The adrenaline that shot through me as I flew acted as a painkiller, so I see the blood but don't feel any pain. It's not a really bad cut. "I do think I need new pants though." I smile at Pete.

"Yeah, we'll get you those. How was your trip? Hahaha!" I can tell Pete is going to be cracking jokes about this for the rest of the day.

Back on property before sundown, I spark my first coal while bow drilling. Once in a while there are good days.

Day 48

I'm on MOB now. That means I'm on my way to becoming a Hawk—and to going home. Or wherever. Since I can't talk, these are my observations:

KASSANDRA

What, you read only the first five pages of your book? Five pages? Come on. I know you can do better than that. You always make good efforts hustling at call time and picking up the slack where others are lacking.

Being inconsiderate doesn't get you anywhere with these girls, especially if you're running down the mountain as if you own it and making Slammer feel not only left out, but nervous and uncomfortable. You did make up for it by helping her out with her trap line.

For you and me, it was harder when we were new, because Christine and Lindsay didn't have any time to help us. We had to figure things out on our own.

But you're acting like a bully, whether you believe it or not, with your snide remarks behind someone's back, or even to her face. You don't need to be that girl anymore. You're a leader of this group. Stop trying to prove something; there's nothing left to prove. Leave Erin alone.

I love you and you're my best friend in this group, but you should understand why Pete won't give you Hawk privileges.

(Hawk privileges are when you acquire the right to know facts that were previously kept from you, such as the time of day, or FI (future information). Maybe you'll find out where we're going for our hike. These are stupid little pieces of information that we grab onto because so much information is withheld.)

(I'm drawn to Kasandra because, unlike the others, she doesn't have a family that's coddling her and making excuses for her. Often she reminds me that she's from the ghetto and her neighborhood is not safe. She has described walking home alone, worrying that someone was going to rob her. Once I asked her how her parents are paying for this wilderness program. It's really expensive. She's getting help from the state or some form of financial aid to send her here. She's more down-to-earth than the other girls, so it's easier to talk to her. And one big thing that we have in common: she shares my wish about getting out of here as quickly as possible. However long it takes.)

We're so close to making it out of here, Kass. Don't screw it up.

RAQUEL

Focus on call. It is not OK what you are doing. Because of you, we have missed five calls in a row for the most idiotic and completely avoidable reasons:

1. Chugging water
2. Putting gear on pack

3. Taking too long to eat breakfast
4. Drinking water
5. Taking too long to eat dinner

This entire set of incidents could have been avoided. The list reveals your carelessness and lack of consideration for the others in the group, who all bust their asses day in and day out to push this group farther so we can all improve and graduate from this program. But we're only as strong as our weakest link, and you've been ours since the day you arrived.

This set of criticism is no different from what I was doing wrong when I was on MOB to Wolf.

On the plus side, you motivate the group by smiling and cracking funny jokes. If the instructors forget to give you your Ritalin, we definitely all know about it when you start bouncing around like a joker in a king's castle.

But your minus side drags us down more than your plus side (off drugs) lifts us up.

SLAMMER

I'm sorry that you hate life. But suck it the fuck up because you aren't going anywhere and you're stuck with us. We don't like this either. And we don't really like you either, but we've gotten over it. You're doing much better with your attitude than you were at first, but you're taking out your frustrations on Erin. Obviously, if you are rude to Erin, she is going to be rude back, and it will be a never-ending cycle. Learn to live with each other, or this is going to be hell for the rest of the time.

Now that you're on MOB, maybe you can silently reflect on everything that's been going on and we can all be peaceful on the outside, if not the inside.

(No one ever uses Slammer's real name. And because of that, I'll never be able to find her after we all get out of here. I know that her nickname is Sam, but I can't figure out her last name. We're never privy to that information.)

SAMANTHA

You're new. You're trying, but you just don't have enough hiking experience to be comfortable, so no one can blame you for walking slowly or needing a break. If you need one, ask. Most likely, someone else does, too, and just isn't saying it for fear of appearing weak. You have an advantage. Because you're new, there's a learning curve and you aren't expected to be a powerhouse on these hikes. You'll become one, though, so don't worry.

You, too, are quite rude to Erin, like everyone else. She's only 14 years old. You're 17. She tells stories of home and this friend and that boy. But we all know that she is embellishing for attention. You know that, and I do. Why poke fun at her? By making up these grandiose stories of home, she's clearly masking whatever it is that's really wrong. Maybe the truth is that she has no stories and she's just trying to fit into this mismatched group of girls in the woods, and this is the way she's trying. Give her a break. You'll be here with her when I'm gone, and then she won't have anyone around to protect her. But you can.

(Samantha is from Long Island. She's a drinker and driver and got into a couple of car accidents with her boyfriend. In high school, she's the wild child who's always getting caught. I assume she's popular because she's always telling me how she was out at a party or getting in trouble in some way with her friends—either caught smoking in the car, or racing in the car with drugs inside, which led to wrapping her new BMW around a tree.)

ERIN

Just because you have stories from home and you like to hear your own voice all the time, doesn't mean that the rest of the girls are willing to listen. I listen because I've taken you under my wing as the little sister I never had. You'll get as much tolerance as you need from me. But not from them.

I've been done with talking about myself to this group for quite some time, and now I'm more than happy to help you. But you need to understand that the other girls don't find your stories so interesting. Stop, or you'll cause arguments, backlash, and resentment. I once had an entire truth circle talk about why the group didn't like me or the way I spoke. My ego and my pride were internally hurt. You don't want that to be you. Learn from my mistakes.

Because you're from Chappaqua, New York, you're constantly talking about your town's "Chappaqueens." That's how you refer to the popular girls back home. But who cares? These girls don't. Neither do the Chappaqueens who weren't your friends anyway. Focus on *now* and the future you, because that's all you'll get from here on out. Your life as you knew it has changed forever. The way you think about things, process situations, react, and interact, has now been altered.

When you're on MOB, you get the VIP treatment of not having to speak (you're actually not allowed to speak); not having to carry any group gear; not participating in calls; and not doing any type of physical or mental work whatsoever. It's your job to observe the group: each girl as an individual, and also the group as a whole. This gives you time to reflect on everyone and then to make use of your observations to work on yourself. For me, MOB is also a time to get away with doing nothing, being exempt from your normal daily activities that demand so much energy. This is supposed to give you perspective. Use it, abuse it, exploit MOB for all it's worth.

Day 49

Still on MOB. Third day in a row. Still watching, waiting. Forever waiting, for what anymore?

"Pack up," yells Brendan, the new instructor. He works well with Pete. But his voice carries farther. "We're moving campgrounds."

Moving is a pain in the ass but at least I don't have to carry any group gear.

What a holding pattern. This is starting to feel like maze with no way out.

Day 50

Still on MOB, which makes me nervous. How much more alone time do I really need to be able to progress to Hawk? Kassandra and Raquel are Hawks already, and Raquel hinted that the three of us are graduating together this week. So why am I being held up? It doesn't make sense. Kassandra got here after Raquel, and Raquel got here a week after I did. I've done everything in my power to do what I think is right, for myself and for the program. I should graduate tomorrow. But I can't while on MOB.

"Hey, girls!" Cara saunters in from the edge of camp. "Raquel, I have a special surprise for you. Grab whatever personal belongings you'd like and let's go down to the infirm."

"Really?" Raquel jumps up, overly excited. "Ahhh!" A squeal so sharp that it could have cracked glass pours out of her as she runs to Cara, not bothering to bring any belongings with her.

A few short steps down the trail and almost out of sight, Cara turns back and calls, "Kassandra, you're coming too. Grab your stuff and hurry up."

I shoot a look over at Kassandra. She's flushed with joy, her shining eyes almost in tears. She gets up, grabs her journal, and dashes after Cara and Raquel.

Everything slows almost to a stop as I stand still and turn my head to Kass. In slow motion with the sound gone, I sit down in silence, alone, watching them all disappear down the path. I know what's going on. They are going to see their parents for the first time in weeks. Empty, shocked, feeling like I've dropped backward into a pool of water, muffling every sound, every emotion, I struggle to feel anything—the feelings I should have, of confusion and betrayal. Instead, I'm numb, crushed. Nothing.

With no one to watch me, I roll my eyes and drop onto the ground and look into the sky.

I used to predict when I thought I'd graduate. I'd calculate, watching the others go through their stages. I'd observe how long it took before they got to see their parents, and how long their Wolf and Hawk stages were, compared to mine. Raquel told us that Cara hinted we were all graduating together. But now it's only the two of them? What did I do so wrong?

My predictions have been wrong, three times now.

Becoming a Hawk is bittersweet. I got what I've been waiting for, but at the cost of not graduating today with Kassandra and Raquel.

Yesterday, when Kass and Raquel got to see their parents, I figured that maybe Cara was saving mine for last. Or for today.

I was wrong, again. And apparently so was Raquel when she told us that we were all graduating together.

What could I have done so drastically wrong to keep myself here for another whole week? Did Cara and my parents decide something different?

Making things worse, no one has yet told me what school I'm going to. Or whether I get to go home for a couple of days before departing for a strange new school. Or if any of my friends get to come witness my long-delayed graduation.

Everything just floats in the air, as if it never needs to be touched. I sit in the woods, robotically doing the same thing over and over again, thinking that what I am doing is on the right track, and pushing ahead as much as possible before the school year starts so I can actually graduate from high school. Could I really be doing it all wrong? And if so, why isn't anyone telling me what to change? I'm not 14; I'm going to be a senior, the most important year of high school before college, and I'm sitting here like a damn prisoner playing with my thumbs while no one allows me to graduate from a program in which I have clearly been working harder than I ever have before. I am no imbecile, and I am not blind, and I know something is wrong. Yet I cannot do one thing about it.

I know my parents well enough to be sure that they very much want me to go to college. So why would they jeopardize that milestone? Six months away from being eighteen, and I am too immature to participate in the decision that will map out the rest of my life? This drastically rigid thinking is uncharacteristic of parents who saw me through Broadway and everything else that I've accomplished over the years; things that people only dream of achieving.

Today something snapped.

Everything that I thought was true might not be true at all. My opinion means nothing here. That is now blatantly clear. All that I can do is to wait passively for the end, whatever that may be.

Day 52

The rain brings calm and a mood of serenity, patience, and tranquility.

With Kassandra gone, now I have only Erin to talk to every day, which is more like giving her therapy than having free discourse. The new girl, Sam, is still cool, but I've been devoting my remaining energy to Erin. Maybe I see a bit of my best friend from home, Megan, in Erin.

Megan is strong and pretty and outgoing, but underneath, she's insecure and she knows it. When we were younger—I remember this like yesterday—she stole a bunch of our friends' lip glosses because her mom wouldn't let her have them. Megan often lied about who she was hanging out with. She'd say, "Yeah, I'm at Melissa's house; we're chilling, let me call you later." Then I'd call another friend to hang out with, like Lauren or Coral, and say, "Yeah, Megan says she's with Melissa, so I guess she bailed on me." They'd laugh and say, "We're with Melissa. Megan's not here." Megan lied to sound cooler.

And that is what she did. She wanted so badly to be accepted that she lied to try to get there. We all knew her lies; we could read through them, but no one could break through to Megan; it was something, someday, that she'd grow out of on her own. (Later in life, she would, and she did.)

Erin has many of Megan's tendencies. Feeling as if I already know a part of her, I can't let her down as I did with Megan, although that was involuntary—I got sent here.

Erin and I are waiting for instructor changeover, both of us sad to see Pete go. I'm listening absently to some story she's telling me about a party she was invited to but then got grounded, so she missed the coolest party of the year. And about how her parents never let her do anything fun; therefore, it must be their fault that she's friendless.

During this long-winded narrative, I'm feeling thankful for the small advantages of instructor changeover, such as new food bags. The new instructors replenish our supplies of cheese, pretzels, and chocolate Swiss Miss for oats. These items fly during expo because they are the most savory snacks we get.

Some new instructor comes along and pitches my food bag for the week right at my head. I check it out to make sure all the goodies are in there, and also to see if maybe they have switched up the "gorp" mixture of dried fruits. They do that now and then, providing us new concoctions of dehydrated fruits.

Tossing my food bag aside, I fill in the free time we have while waiting for the familiar suburbans to pick us up and drop us at the trailhead for what will hopefully be my last expo.

I grab out my bow drilling set and put it down, still listening to Erin rambling on, and start drilling hard, right into the cedar. I go through a hole a day now bow drilling, yet still no glowing coal. I hope this is one of those things like bike riding, where once you get it, you get it forever. I'm so close to busting a coal. All the punk is black, and I don't think I could drill harder if I tried.

Erin blabbers on and I strike and push hard into the wood. Once I spark a coal I can at least radio Pete and tell him I accomplished it. That's the only perk of sparking a coal. You get to radio your favorite instructor. Something to work for in this last week.

Fire! Finally. Out of my punk.

And Sarah is back. Maybe fire and Sarah have something in common? As in, once they start, it's hard stopping them...

"Sarah," I yell across camp, "Get the radio! We are radioing every instructor and telling them I busted a fire. It has been damn long enough! Phew."

"Congrats! I knew you could," she says. "I was hard on you for a reason." She grabs the radio and hands it over with a smack on my back.

"Adirondack Leadership Expedition Teams," I shriek through the radio. "This is Marissa from team Cartoon (Sarah named us a few expos ago), and I just busted my first fire!"

A few responses come through from instructors I don't even know, congratulating me.

"Where's Pete?" I look over at Sarah.

"He's off camp for the week, but I promise I will tell him you busted the coal when he gets back."

"Now that you've finished all your Hawk skills and you're out on expo, why not try for Hawk with Honors?" she suggests.

"What's that?"

"Only one person has ever graduated from ALE as Hawk

with Honors." That strikes a chord in my competitive nature. I want to be the only girl to ever graduate with honors. "You have to do a few more skills in order to qualify," she explains. "You need to learn compass skills, and then lead a hike bush-whacking with only a map and a compass. And you have to carry a survival pack."

"Survival pack?"

"Yes. Instead of wearing your regular pack, you leave that behind and wrap all your stuff inside your tarp. Then you take the ropes you use for tying up your tent. You tie them around the tarp in a certain manner, securing it all inside. The way you tie it creates holes for your arms to go through, so you can carry it on your back."

The compass idea sounds fine. But that survival pack sounds intense.

"Fine. I'll do it," I answer with conviction.

"After you guide us to our next campsite tomorrow, we'll drop your pack and teach you how to create the survival pack."

"Cool, I'll be ready when you are."

Sarah hands me my new tools. "Here is a compass, a map, and instructions. Look it over, and tomorrow we head out on your first survival hike."

Day 54

Teaching myself how to use a compass worked out fairly well yesterday. But out here, bushwhacking through unforgiving terrain, we can conclude that I'm no expert at compass skills.

Though I do, in the end, hike us to a lean-to! Best of all, this one has an actual outhouse, equipped with a door for privacy and all. It's the first that I've seen here at ALE. Everywhere else, even if we had a lean-to to sleep in, we had to dig cat holes for toilets. Every single time. It's one of the most disgusting aspects of this whole experience. Now I can leisurely walk out past the camp a bit to the enclosed wooden Porta-Potty lookalike.

"Packs on, girls, today isn't over yet," Sarah yells across camp. "Oh, day packs, we're staying at this campsite. Five minutes!" She smiles and goes to sit in the center of base camp, waiting for us all to gather around.

I guess the first part of my hike wasn't enough for today, so we get to hike up yet another mountain, hopefully a small one, maybe McKenzie Mountain? I saw it on the map while hiking to the lean-to this morning.

SOME HOURS LATER AT THE SUMMIT

I was wrong in my assumptions. We hiked up Mount Haystack, which wasn't much different on the map from McKenzie; it was just steeper, which is more fun when it becomes an obstacle course. All of the things that used to be so excruciating to me before, like hiking up mountains, are no longer intimidating. Continuing the day with not just one but two hikes has now become routine, mundane even.

I just follow blindly and have learned to let it all go. My friends are gone, I am still here, and they still do not know where I'm going after I leave. Or that's what they're saying. My time is running short.

Sitting at the summit of Haystack, I look out over the terrain we just encountered and breathe a sigh of relief that we are not allowed to sit by ourselves up here to think. Swirling in my mind are ideas about last-ditch efforts to get home. If they're never going to let me graduate, what else can I do besides escape?

I don't really care about smoking pot, which is one of the reasons I ended up here. It was never an escape from reality for me, just a bonding experience with the kids in my grade. Smoking a blunt or a joint that has to be passed around for 10 to 20 minutes forces kids who wouldn't otherwise talk to each other, to now engage in conversation.

I made friends this way. This helped my social life in so many ways, which my parents didn't see. They think I'm addicted to a drug that's holding me back, when really I received more apologies from all sorts of kids in school this year because they had the time to sit down and talk to me. And it was the weed that slowed them down. They were sorry about the way they'd treated me during freshman year. Forced conversation. And it helped me so much.

I was once a kid who was mercilessly teased for everything. Anything about me was fuel for their bullying, from the sound of my voice, to kids just being vindictive and calling me a whore. I'd never even seen a penis my freshman year! I used to walk down the hallways pretending I didn't hear while upper-class girls called out "Dumb Slut" because of a stupid video some dumb AV kids made of me when I was a freshman.

They picked on me for what should be considered good things—my talents. I was in the school play, and because of my acting history, I got a good part. That meant that the senior who wanted that part lost her last chance to get a good role in a school play. Well, they picked me. I just auditioned like everybody else. I obviously wasn't doing this to hurt anyone. I didn't ask for the part; I just received it.

At the cast party after the last show, two kids whose names no one even knew were carrying around video cameras to film everything. They were considered "AV kids." No one paid much attention; they were just referred to as "those creepy kids." I've told you this story before, but now I'm sitting here on top of this mountain, thinking it over from a new perspective.

My mom finally let me go to the cast party, where these two creepy kids asked to see my bellybutton ring, so I showed them. Bad judgment! Brooke, the girl whose house I was supposed to sleep at that night, was too drunk to go home. So she asked me if we could stay out longer with the boys until she sobered up, so her mom wouldn't get angry. I said fine, no biggie.

This turned into a five-hour ordeal of driving around in the hills of our town, with the boys asking me over and over to show them my boobs and so on. They threatened that if

I didn't, they wouldn't drive me home. But I never showed them anything besides my bellybutton ring.

Finally they drove me home, but the story didn't end there. On Monday morning, there was a video on the Internet titled "Dumb Slut," featuring me. They had taken the shot of me showing my bellybutton ring and cut the camera, writing a caption that read "Only for our eyes," implying that I took my shirt off. Which I never did. They took a video of me walking, and captioned that, "If she walks a certain number of miles, she will work the jizz calories off," implying that I'd given someone a blowjob. I was 14. I'd never even seen a penis, let alone done anything that these jerks were implying.

Three years later, when I was a junior, half the school apologized to me for the cruelty they'd subjected me to. And that was all because they'd finally got to sit down with me and talk to me while we were sharing a joint. Talking and being friendly, as opposed to yelling shit at me as I walked past in school.

That's over and done. Now that most people see the real me, I don't even care about smoking anymore. I'll sign a contract with my parents allowing them to randomly drug-test me, whatever they want. I just want to go home for my senior year. That's all. If they still don't know where to place me, maybe there is still time? It's my 54th day out here and they still don't know? That's absurd anyway.

Maybe if I write a compelling letter and a "contract" of sorts giving them all the authority they want, maybe they will reconsider?

It feels like the woods are turning into my home, with no light at the end of a long tunnel. It's been so long. I just want to go home.

Day 55

We're hiking up a mountain today. Because I am now a Hawk, the instructors aren't hiding so many facts from me anymore. They showed me the map, which told me the peak is around 1185 feet high. This seems to be a bit less steep than yesterday's climb, and it's a day hike, which is great.

I don't have to start using my survival pack until we leave the lean-to, which I believe will be tomorrow. I hope we go back to property after tonight so I can work on writing a contract to my parents. Why would they want to waste money on a boarding school if I am going to sign myself out at 18 anyway?

I was told that these boarding schools we're all getting sent to are for minors. Our parents sign our rights over, much as they did to send us here to ALE. But once we hit 18, we are not minors anymore, and our lives are in our hands.

So I have already decided that I won't spend one day longer in an institution than I absolutely have to. Come February 24, 2007, my eighteenth birthday, I will be out of there. Which is right in the middle of the school year anyway. If I go home then, I will be sober; I'll give that to my parents. But the only thing I can give myself is freedom, once I have the ability to do so.

They don't need to know that yet. If it turns out that I have no choice, that I am going somewhere against my will, I will let them know what I choose to do on my birthday. Maybe they'll think it's a waste and bring me home. Or maybe they'll cut me off the minute I sign myself out, and leave me out in the cold. Stranger things have happened.

What, I wonder, does all of this mean for my senior year of high school?

There's a contradiction here: from the moment you step into middle school, all of the forces groom you to enter a great college. These include your teachers, your parents, your friends, your friends' parents, and the town itself. My life has been no exception to that tradition.

With that in mind, how can a therapeutic boarding school possibly offer a good educational program if all of its students were sent there for behavior problems? In general, good grades and behavior problems do not go hand in hand.

Whether anyone here or my parents believe I still have problems that need to be worked out, there is no denying that I have always been a good student. So what happens to college now?

Day 1 of the survival pack.

Sarah clips my empty pack to her backpack so we can get going with my extra Hawk requirements before we return to property. I guess Hawk with Honors is a big deal for them.

It's a big deal for me, too. I always want to be the best at something. My first goal was to graduate at 28 days, which would have broken a record, but I came nowhere near doing that. So now I'm focusing on this new goal because no girl has ever graduated as Hawk with Honors. I'm feeling pretty cool; better at being in the woods than the others. I feel like the main person in my group.

They've granted me the privilege of knowing that this is our last day on expo before we go back to camp tomorrow. Sarah whispered it to me as she was showing me how to tie my survival pack together correctly. I suppose it was her way of trying to make me smile, knowing I was going to be walking around with this weird homemade backpack for a few miles.

When I first met Sarah, she was difficult to read and get along with. My first impression of her is an image stamped into my memory: she was screaming at me to keep on doing pack drills, antagonizing me, wearing me down to the point where I considered not moving altogether, coming to a total standstill as Molly did, way back when.

Then she got a bit easier when she brought her good-natured dog Shadow along on one expo. She seemed somewhat more human with this dog that she loved and cared for. In fact, seeing Sarah with Shadow was a stark opposite of that first negative impression.

Now Sarah and I can converse calmly. I'm no longer projecting any anger on her because at this point I know, and have fully accepted, that I am here, and that it was not she who put me here. It is also not her decision when I leave or where I go after this.

If I ever get out of here… it's the middle of August already. Stray leaves are gliding off the trees now and then, forecasting autumn, the season of new academic beginnings, and I'm still here, waiting.

"Ready to put this on?" Sarah smiles as our final touches tie onto the pack.

"Yep, let's go." With a hard swing and a little assistance, I hoist the uncomfortable pack on my back, and we're off to a new campsite.

Back to hiking and thinking. After Kassandra graduated, I took Erin under my wing and I've also been helping some of the newer girls. I've been told that I'm a bit bossy. I can see this. I am.

My goals for today, besides the survival pack, were written for me by another instructor:

1. Hike with survival pack.
2. You do not always need to put your two cents in!
3. The group needs everyone, not just you.

At least I've progressed from crying and useless to way too helpful. Bright side?

Yesterday I got more practice with my survival pack, part of my Hawk with Honors requirements. Besides getting out of here, graduating Hawk with Honors is my highest priority, and I'm giving it all I've got. Under my heavy burden, I kept up with the group as we hiked to a campsite close to where the black suburbans would pick us up.

Now all the girls in my group are piling into the suburbans, one by one. The cars drive through the property marker and right up to the infirm. We never pay much attention to who's driving, and we never know their names. They have remained faceless my entire stay here.

Following our normal routine, each girl rolls out of the car in turn, monotonously, until we're all standing there waiting for orders. Everything is the same as it's ever been, except for one thing: I see a figure off in the distance, maybe Cara, standing by the infirm's back stairs. That's where new campers usually go for the intake procedure.

"Grab your packs and pick a spot to have lunch by the benches." One of the instructors herds us toward the wooden benches outside the infirm. "We're having our sessions with Cara right here."

Grabbing my survival pack from the back of the car is less

of a strain on my shoulders than it was during yesterday's hike. There are no arm straps, just the ropes we use to tie our tents at night, wrapped around in intricate designs, tightening all my belongings together. The strings feel like they're ripping through your shirt to your skin with no padding. After a while your shoulders form thicker skin, creating their own padding, the way calluses form on your hands and fingers.

One by one, we all plop down in front of the benches. As usual, we turn around to the top portion of our packs to undo the latch where our food bags are hidden away. With this survival pack, I have no latches or zippers, so I find an open spot on the grass to set down my pack, and I undo the entire thing. Tie after tie, twist after twist of ropes, I open the tarp containing my stuff and shuffle through for my food bag, which is smaller than usual, since this is the last day or so I'll have this food bag. I quickly snatch the bag and then pull my blue tarp lightly over my things without retying everything. Then I flip around onto my back looking straight up into the sky, and there's Cara standing right in my line of sight.

"You're graduating on Thursday!" she announces. Shooting upright, I cannot believe my ears. I knew I would get out of here eventually, I guess, but hearing it for real almost feels like a cruel joke. Flashback to Raquel telling me and Kass that we were all graduating together. But this time is for real. I can feel my heart thumping.

Cara smiles. "You and I are going to meet last today so I can explain everything to you." She walks away and calls Erin.

"Wait, wait, don't go away!" I yell after her. Standing up fast and excited, I scream, "Wait, wait, why can't we meet now?" But these words are lost, and Cara is already back by the infirm stairs.

Holy shit. I'm graduating on Thursday. That's the day after tomorrow. I sit back down and let my back drop onto the ground and breathe a giant, cleansing sigh of relief. This is it. This is what I've been waiting for. I get to sleep in a bed soon. I get to see and talk to other people. Normal people, not in captivity. Even boys! I get to leave—but not go home. So is this really the end? I sit here on the ground, waiting for my turn with Cara. Thoughts about my immediate future are doing loops around my brain like a plane in a holding pattern.

After Cara has seen all the other girls, one by one, it's finally my turn. "You are going to Academy at Swift River," she tells me with no introduction. I can hardly pay attention to the words, but at first hearing, the name sounds promising. Anticipating my question, she says, "It's around the Berkshires near Northampton in Massachusetts."

Nowhere near home in New Jersey. I'm going straight there after my parents pick me up, she says. No home visit first. No time to reconnect with my friends. It's like I don't get a chance to be the self I used to be, before I move into yet another place and learn how to be the self my parents want me to be, or the program will want me to be.

Cara shows me a brochure. "This is the school your parents decided on."

In one photo, a few kids are smiling in their polo shirts and khakis—their uniform, it appears—in front of a white building with green-edged windows, very New England preppy-looking. At least it's coed. Before Cara snatches the brochure away, I read, "Helping kids get back on track by restoring relationships..." Which relationships? I don't know anyone in this place. How can they restore relationships that never existed?

"There are only 100 kids there," she says. "It's a college preparatory school. Your parents chose this one because they still want you to have a chance at college."

A chance? All along, I'd thought it was guaranteed that I'd go to college.

Before I can ask her anything, she says, "It's minimally therapeutic." As opposed to what, I wonder? "And it's not considered a lockdown."

Thoughts along the lines of *maybe this won't be so bad* suddenly change to feelings of dread and foreboding. I can't know this now, but I'll find out in time that the therapy at Swift River is pretty intense. And forget about not being locked in. If you try to leave, they bring you back by any means possible.

Now the meeting is over, and all my unanswered questions will have to wait. We're sleeping out under the stars tonight, not under tarps, and we're all right next to each other. Having company, practically any kind of company, is comforting at a time like this. So many unknowns are out there waiting for me. And none of them are under my control or of my own choosing. Tomorrow is my first meeting with my parents in two months. I finally fall asleep, apprehensive about my new destination, and still holding onto a fragment of hope.

Day 58

I'm stewing in a brew of the most uneasy, awkward emotions I've ever experienced, anywhere. All of the milestone events that might trouble or worry other people never bothered me. That includes the usual collection of childhood and adolescent challenges, such as exams, team tryouts, and oral reports; as well as some unusual ones, like auditions for commercials and acting roles, even on Broadway. But I feel myself shaking as I follow Cara up the stairs to where I was first interviewed by a stone-faced woman on Day 1. My parents are up there now in that bare room, waiting for me.

"Mom. Hi. Dad." I just stare at them. I can feel tears start to roll down my cheeks once again; something I haven't done in a while now. Cry. I'd forgotten the point of crying. Oh, I did plenty of that when I first ended up here, but it didn't do me any good. There they are, standing together, just looking at me. I look back into their faces and I can see my mother's eyes starting to water as well. I don't want to give them the satisfaction of seeing me cry. But I cannot help it. It's been so long. I am so hurt by them. But right now, they are the only ones who can take me away from this place. I'm struggling with a mixture of elation, relief, anger, and disgust, all at the same time.

They're looking at me, standing here in front of them in ALE's trademark bright-red pants and orange fleece, holding some of my beaten-up journals. I wonder if it's hit them yet—where I actually am. What I have been doing here for eight long weeks. How traumatic it was, the night they had me taken. Do they know? Do they care? I'm not sure.

My mom reaches out for a hug and embraces me, and I hug her back, just like a little girl, feeling vulnerable after all these weeks of toughing it out in the woods. We're not a hugging, demonstrative kind of family. We'll have our perfunctory hugs at appropriate moments, but our familial love isn't measured in affectionate gestures.

She holds me by the arms (my stronger, harder biceps) and says, "You look good! How are you! What's been going on? Are you excited to leave?" she sputters out almost in one sentence.

Dad gives me a quick hug. "Have you learned some stuff? What did they teach you?" he asks.

I look around and don't answer. "Where's Golan?"

"We don't know, Marissa. We don't know where he is," my mom says. "Megan and I have been talking and I've been giving her all your letters. She says that she and all your girlfriends have been reading them together." She counts friends on her fingers, "Megan, Lauren, Matt, Lindsay, and Golan. She doesn't know if he's left for Israel yet."

"Why couldn't they come?"

"It's best to have a family session," Cara interjects.

I shoot Cara a look, the kind of look I haven't dared give anyone of authority in this place, and repeat the question to my parents. "Why couldn't they come?"

Mom tries to offer a better response, but it sounds the same as Cara's, only more long-winded: "We thought it would be better to have some family time before you go off to your new school, and we wanted to make the most out of it."

Before I go off to my new school. As if it's my idea to get stuck in some therapeutic boarding school with another bunch of troubled teenagers. It's my friends that I want, my friends that I've been missing, and they're not here.

Mom smiles. "When we leave and go into town, we can get your hair done, and do some shopping for school, and you can have your phone to call all your friends."

"OK." My phone. My own real phone, with my life on it—all my friends' numbers, and some pictures, too.

My parents sit down in the same place where P was sitting when I entered this room for intake, two long months ago. I do the same and sit in the same spot where I asked P my first questions, which remained unanswered. And the three of us start to talk, covering all the acceptable topics: the skills I've learned, the program lessons, descriptions of hikes I went on, and mountains I climbed.

But there are still certain questions I need to ask. "I thought I was graduating last week with Raquel and Kassandra? What happened?" I ask all of them.

"Who?" My mother tilts her head.

"Two girls that I've been in the program with for a while. Doesn't matter. But Raquel said we were all leaving together. Why did I have to stay?"

"Well, we weren't sure which school was best," my father says.

Oh, so they kept me here because it was convenient, so they could vacillate about schools and my future.

"We looked at a bunch of schools, including the ones Ben Mason suggested after your meeting with him. We even visited some," my mother says.

Ben Mason was the boarding school consultant I met about two or three weeks ago, but I couldn't draw any conclusions after that meeting. "What about San Bernardino, and California, and the pre-professional school?" I ask them desperately.

"Your grades were not good enough," my father says blankly.

"But my junior year was my only off year for grades; other than that, my entire GPA has always been a 3.5 or higher!" I plead.

"Well, with your junior year dropping to 2.7, it didn't matter that freshman and sophomore year were 3.8s because you needed a 3.5 to get in," my mother says.

"And you didn't have that when we inquired about getting you in there," my father says, sounding angry about my GPA.

But that's not all it takes to get into a pre-professional school! They know it, and I know it. "You couldn't do anything?" I practically scream at them. "I've been a child actor since age seven. I'm in Screen Actors Guild, AFTRA, and Actors Equity!" I grip the table and lean in. "They didn't care about my talents? They cared more about my grades?" I'm trying as hard as I can to stop this train before it wrecks, but I know this is a lost cause. They've clearly made up their minds.

"No, they simply would not accept you," my father says in a tone of voice that indicates he's wrapping this up.

I didn't even get the chance to apply, I think. *I didn't get to go to the interview, or to audition, or to write my essay...*

"We chose Swift River because it's only a couple hours away from us if you need to come home or for us to visit you," my mom says. "And the dress requirements aren't that bad. Just polos and khakis."

"I don't even own a pair of khakis."

"We'll find some."

"You were not brought here to talk to your parents about a boarding school you didn't get into or the clothing you will be wearing," Cara barks. "This is a time for you guys to talk before your graduation. In a mediated format."

Fuck your psychobabble. I'm out of here tomorrow, and I'll never see you again.

"Great. Have any other questions for me?" I ask. "I'm still graduating Hawk with Honors, right?

"Yes, you should." Cara smiles, that fake smile, feeling that order has been restored. "Nothing else then?"

No one moves or says anything. I can't believe my parents are putting up with her stupid restrictions, just accepting them without question.

"So I guess I'll see you tomorrow, then?" Standing up, I give each of my parents a quick hug, and walk out of that room for the last time.

AFTER DINNER, BACK AT CAMPSITE

My last night here... I'm sitting alone, thinking, wondering about the future.

"Pack drills, everyone! To your tents!" Sarah cries out.

"What?" I look at Sarah. Stare at her. Almost testing her to see if this is just a cruel joke.

"Pack drills, Marissa. I know your first time with them was rough, but over the weeks, you've gotten great at it. What's the problem?"

"I have a survival pack. Not an actual pack. I can't do a pack drill in three minutes while having to tie all my stuff together with all those knots." I'm still frozen in place, staring at Sarah.

"You don't have a choice," she snaps. "Everyone else has to do them, and so do you. You're a Hawk with Honors now. You can't just refuse to do what everyone else is doing. I thought you were a leader, Marissa."

"I am a leader of this group, but this is just ridiculous," I complain. "And cruel. The night before I'm leaving?"

"What's a pack drill?" Erin pops her head out from behind me.

I explain to her, "It's a stupid drill they make us do where

we have to tear down our personal campsite and pack everything into our bag in less than three minutes, and be ready to
hike." I'm yelling at her as if she's the cause of all this. What a
case of misplaced aggression. "It wastes time, and we all hate
it."

Erin, realizing that I'm starting to lose it, backs away to
her tent close to mine and sits down to watch.

I pivot to Sarah and declare, "I'm not doing a pack drill
with a survival pack the night before leaving, in the dark! I've
done more than enough for this program, and dealt with all
of this crap. Now you are going to throw this at me, when
you know it's extremely difficult. What for? So you can have
some fun with me before I leave?" My body is flushed with
heat, tears well up in my eyes, and the rage from within is
starting to reach the surface. Trying hard to suck it down,
taking deep breaths, clenching my firsts, and standing firm, I
wait for Sarah to answer.

"This is not the behavior of a Hawk with Honors,
Marissa," she scolds. "You might not be able to graduate
tomorrow if you don't cooperate."

"I've done everything for you," I say, raising my voice. "I
learned the compass. I hiked with this makeshift piece-of-shit
survival pack. I've literally bled for this program. What more
do you want from me? I am a Hawk with Honors regardless
of this moronic pack drill."

Erin is whispering from behind me. "Marissa, please. I
want you to go home. You don't know what they could do to
you, or tell your parents."

Sam chimes in, "I've seen you be so strong since the day I
got here, and you've helped me with my acceptance of being
here. You can't give up now."

"Marissa, it's a pack drill, suck it up," Slammer says in her
most encouraging voice.

From across camp, I can see the other instructors radioing

Cara on the satellite to let her know about the situation. Hand motions all around are signaling distress, showing that the instructors clearly don't know what to do. Their lips form the words, "What do we do with her?"

Now panic is starting to spread throughout camp, in the girls' eyes and the instructors' eyes. In Sarah, especially. Sarah, who had become somewhat of a friend to me, the way Pete was when he was here. No one knows what to do. As they see it, my episode of rebelliousness couldn't have been predicted. In real life, I am unpredictable, but this isn't my real life. These people have not seen the real Marissa—until now. In the wilderness, I have been calculated since the day I got here, and this is wildly out of character. No wonder they're so nervous.

My stern self-control has snapped. Tears stream down my face uncontrollably as all the built-up emotions break loose. I'm breaking down because of the 58 days I've been stuck here; because I met my parents for the first time in so long; because my graduation from this miserable program will be followed by yet another exile far from home. Tears. Tears and heat. I am so physically hot. My skin is burning.

There's no exit from these oppressors. "Let's get this over with," I finally say to Sarah in a low voice.

I miss call number one, but I finish the second time, struggling with the ropes, the weight, and all those intricate ties. Once all of us are done, we set up our camp again, right in the same spot where we took it down. We're not even moving campsite. It's just another punitive exercise in busywork. I'm seething with fury that I'm not allowed to express.

This has been their last test for me. And I failed. I find out that I'm not going to graduate Hawk with Honors. They took it away from me. The last thing they could take away, after my privacy, my dignity, and my right to self-determination, they took.

Graduation

My parents aren't saying much. They're sitting here on benches, watching what ALE calls a graduation ceremony. I'm the only one graduating today, but the other girls are participating, each one demonstrating some wilderness skill. My skill is bow drilling, although I can't manage to spark a fire with all of them watching. I try twice.

Pete is here just for my graduation, and I'm glad I get to see him before leaving. He's one of the few people here who made the whole experience almost bearable. With his comments like, "I'd have tried certain drugs, too," and his helpful advice, such as how to make our own bridge out of people to cross the lake to the lean-to at Whiteface Mountain. I wish he could be my friend after here, or that I could somehow find him after boarding school.

When the formalities are over, they hand me my certificate of completion, which says, sure enough, "Hawk," not "Hawk with Honors." One more stab on the way out. I don't show the anger building inside me from that insult. But the fact is that I worked for that distinction. I deserved it, and they took it away. True, I had a bit of a breakdown last night when I did not want to do pack drills with my survival pack. But come on, seriously. Hawk with Honors was the only goal left for me to strive and work for, once I was told I wasn't going home. It was something in the program that I actually, truly got into, a challenge that I liked, that worked for me. I diligently met all the requirements, and then they took away my hard-earned title. It's a piece of paper. Couldn't they just have made me smile on my graduation day?

Overwhelmed by emotions I do not know how to show, I appear stoic; though beneath the surface is turbulence; that's the only word for it. I want desperately to know where my friends are. Don't parents understand that teenagers' peers are a vital reflection of their own developing identities? What happened to my friends? My life literally stopped on June 20 when those two thugs broke into my bedroom in the middle of the night and took me away. Now, two months later and almost time for senior year, I don't know what everyone is doing or where they are. Or if Golan is still in the country.

My friends are a main concern, but not so much my parents' wellbeing. They're here and I can see that they're fine. Regardless of what they did to me, they're still my parents and I'm happy to see them. And of course, they're my key to leaving the woods and returning to civilization.

Hardest to deal with is my anger, a type of anger I've never felt before. I'm so angry that after all this punishment and sacrifice, I'm not going home, not even for a weekend visit. The phrase "therapeutic boarding school" conjures up an image of an institution where it's them against us—authorities who act like they know what's best for us, against us teenagers whose parents have abandoned us to this asylum.

All these errant thoughts are fluttering through my mind as the graduation winds up. Holding the certificate that says that I'm free, but not good enough, I hug each girl goodbye. In spite of their problems and attitudes, I care about all of them, each one, and I'm going to miss them. I wish them well, and I mean it, from the heart.

I say goodbye to Sarah, my tormentor, forcing myself to be polite even though she took away my Honors distinction in a last act of domination. We get it, Sarah, you're the big badass counselor on campus. And I hug Pete and thank him for being a great instructor. I walk away, loaded down with as much of my stuff as I can carry, and knowing that I'm never coming back.

Then, the moment I've dreamed of during all those interminable, sweaty hikes: for the first time in more than eight weeks, my family and I are together. We walk down the dirt road and up to the infirm. I climb into the backseat of our family car.

As we drive away, I change my clothes right there. I change quickly, not caring about who's in the car; I'm used to changing in tight spots, from all my years of acting, where you constantly have to improvise places to dress in a hurry. My mom packed a few of my summer clothes, like jeans and tops, and I toss my filthy red and orange wilderness clothes on the floor and dive into something more comfortable and less smelly. I was slim to begin with, but now the waistband of my jeans is really loose. In my own real clothes, sitting here with my parents up front, I feel like the real me is taking over. To tell the truth, the real me got a head start yesterday, which ended up costing me my Hawk with Honors distinction. Whoops.

Now it's all behind me. I hope. I don't want to live a life of flashbacks after this. The changing scenery is helping. We're driving out of the Adirondacks and into Connecticut, and we're going to stop about an hour away from Cummington, Massachusetts, where my new school is located. One more small adventure into a real town before the school doors shut behind me.

As soon as the landscape levels off, my mom hands me my precious cell phone and I start calling all my friends right away; Megan first, of course. Hearing her voice is like getting a cool drink of water after a long, hard hike under the blazing sun. I've been so thirsty for her company and her friendship. I cry and call all of my girlfriends, who are also crying on the other end, so happy to hear my voice, and that I'm alive and intact—not eaten by a bear, they laugh.

My dad pulls into a motel parking lot in the Berkshires, and we unload the car. I bring in my clothes, journals, bow drilling set, hiking stick, and everything else I took away with me. This stuff is all important to me. I feel attached to most of it. It's what I've worked on for the past eight weeks and I don't want to part with any of it.

But my parents comment on the odor of my belongings, especially my clothes. To me, they barely smell like anything at all—the woods, fire, sweat, that sort of thing. I insist, and they let me keep them.

Before we go out to dinner at a real restaurant, I take a long, hot, soapy shower, using up two of those little motel soap bars and a generous handful of my mother's fragrant shampoo. The wide, well-lit bathroom mirror shows a tight, muscular body with no spare fat in sight. This one, I consider a win. Any baby fat I had before has certainly melted away, and most of the mosquito bites I got during the first few weeks are gone. I look great. This is awesome. Refreshed.

The food in the restaurant is delicious. I order filet mignon and fancy side dishes, but of course, my stomach isn't used to this kind of food, or so much of it, either, and I can barely manage to eat half of what I ordered.

Our motel room is a suite, with a double bed for me in a separate room. I plop down in the middle of the bed with my cell phone, finishing the calls I started in the car. Until I get too tired to keep my eyes open, I spend the entire time talking to my friends from home, who have THOUSANDS of questions. I don't know if my parents are listening, and I don't care. I'm sure they don't mind what I'm talking about. I'm not planning an escape, although I did give out the address of my new school to all my friends, just in case they want to drop by some day.

It's nice to be in a soft, big, clean bed, wearing clean clothes, with dry hair, no tarp, and no bugs. But it feels quiet, strange, and somehow artificial. And so very far from home.

The next day, we go shopping around town, where my mom promises to get me everything I need for school. I try on khakis, shirts, even underwear. Khakis are ugly, but they're better than my orange prison pants. Mom and I notice how my body is better than it was before ALE. I have more muscle and less fat. Remember, I haven't been allowed to look in a mirror all this time, so this shopping experience is a revelation. I keep joking with my mom that at least ALE gave me a great body.

My attitude is, OK, go ahead, I'll let you buy me whatever I want, and you can pay for me to color my hair. The beauty makeover is exciting. This hairdresser must be wondering what happened to me—when I walked in, my hair was all brown on top and then faded into the light blonde it was at the time I was taken. It's a great pleasure to watch all my raggedy split ends tumble to the floor. During wilderness, my hair stopped growing on the right side, probably for some stress-related reason. As she combs through my hair, the hairdresser asks me why one side is longer than the other. I laugh and tell her that my hair fell out. This is not a normal response from a 17-year-old. Healthy teenagers' hair does not just split and fall out for no reason. It was stress that my body reacted to in a weird way.

At least, I'm letting my parents pamper me for this brief interlude between two custodial institutions. We have three days total together before I'm shipped away again. After wilderness, I don't care at all about their money or their wishes for me. I'm focused on myself, and getting there, where the new goal is, in my mind: *Marissa, you're OK until 18. Just wait until you're 18.*

I love my parents for trying to make these three days as pleasant as possible. We don't discuss much about where I am going. I'm not sure they even know the details of the program in this school where they're dropping me.

On the 18th of August, 2006, I enter The Academy at Swift River. It's going to be a quick goodbye. My parents escort me into a kind of all-purpose corridor. Taking a quick look around at a few students there, my first reaction is that they seem robotic, fake, with no discernible emotions. Oh, do I hope I'm wrong.

About five seconds after I hug my parents goodbye, one of the men in charge, whoever he is, motions for me to follow him. "Come with me, Marissa," he invites me. "I'll show you around."

None of the kids look at me for more than a second, as their eyes quickly return to whatever they are doing.

"Don't worry about them," the man says, and pats me on the back. "They're just doing their after-breakfast chores."

I shoot a quick glance behind me to where my parents and I entered the facility. The door shuts, and now they are gone.

Deep, long breaths, as it starts again.

Six months until I turn 18.

Made in United States
North Haven, CT
29 May 2023

37122391R00150